The Soup Book

'Soup-making is one of the most pleasurable of culinary processes, but it takes time, and that is perhaps why it is so little enjoyed in a hurried age. The widespread use of tinned foods, such a boon to arctic explorers and working wives, has served to lessen the numbers of practitioners of this art. My hope in compiling this little book is to persuade those who read it that the soup you make yourself is infinitely superior to soup from a packet or tin, and that making soup is a comforting activity, surpassed only by the activity of eating it.'

Cooks are once again realising the great value of home-made soups, not just for their nourishment, but because they are delicious and wonderfully versatile. Carolyn McCrum gives clear advice on basic methods, stocks and equipment. Her recipes are practically divided into sections such as 'Main Course Soups' for family suppers, cool and refreshing 'Summer Soups', and 'Time-Saving Soups' for emergencies.

CAROLYN McCRUM

The Soup Book

MAGNUM BOOKS
Methuen Paperbacks Ltd

A Magnum Book

THE SOUP BOOK
ISBN 0 417 02970 5

First published 1978 by Magnum Books

Copyright © 1978 Carolyn McCrum

Magnum Books are published by
Methuen Paperbacks Ltd
11 New Fetter Lane, London EC4P 4EE

Made and printed in Great Britain by
Hazell Watson & Viney Ltd
Aylesbury, Bucks

All the line drawings in *The Soup Book* are reproduced by kind permission of The Mary Evans Picture Library.

Contents

Introduction

SOUP-MAKING IS ONE OF THE most pleasurable of culinary processes, but it takes time, and that is perhaps why it is so little enjoyed in a hurried age. The widespread use of tinned foods, such a boon to arctic explorers and working wives, has served to lessen the numbers of practitioners of this art. My hope in compiling this little book is to persuade those who read it that the soup you make yourself is infinitely superior to soup from a packet or tin, and that making soup is a comforting activity, surpassed only by the activity of eating it.

The English word 'soup', defined as 'a liquid food prepared by boiling, usually consisting of an extract of meat with other ingredients and seasoning', dates back to 1653. It is derived from the French 'soupe', which in Cassell's French Dictionary is 'soup; sop (soaked slices of bread); food, grub, signal for dinner.'

The evolution of soup was of great interest to 'the King of Chefs', Auguste Escoffier, who tells us that 'the nutritious liquids known under the name of Soups are of comparatively recent origin. Indeed, as they are now served, they do not date any further back than the early years of the nineteenth century. The soups of old cookery were, really, complete dishes, wherein the meats and vegetables used in their preparations were assembled. Modern cookery has replaced those stodgy dishes of yore by comparatively simple and savoury preparations which are veritable wonders of delicacy and taste.'

Recipes for something resembling soup appeared in the earliest printed cookery book, *Platine De Honesta Voluptate Et Valetudine*. It chiefly contained sauces, soups and stews, as the fork had not been invented, and these could all be eaten with a spoon. The author, Bartholomeo Sicci, was Librarian to the Vatican City, and his study of cooking, eating and drinking not only encouraged the cooks of his day, but also reassured those whose Christian consciences might have stood in the way of a serious study of food and wine.

There are few references to either vegetables or fruits in early English cookery books, but cabbage was mentioned in the 15th century as an ingredient for soup. Among the items on the menu of a Brewers' Company grand dinner in 1419 was 'caboges to the potage'.

The Compleat Housewife appeared in the 18th century to guide the diligent cook. In addition to recipes, this marvel offered menus for every month of the year. 'Soop' appears to have become an established part of the first course, as a sample January menu shows:

First Course	*Second Course*
Soop à-la-royal	Woodcocks
Carp Blovon	Pheasants
Tench stewed with pitch-cocked eels	Salmigondi
Rump of beef à la braise	Bisque of lamb
Turkeys à la daube	Oyster loaves
Wild ducks comporte	Cutlets
Fricando of veal with veal olives	Pippins stewed

It is perhaps not widely known that soup was instrumental in the founding of the first restaurant as such. In 18th century France, one could dine out only in inns or at the shops of the traiteurs (eating-house keepers), who as members of a corporation were allowed to offer set pieces to the public. In 1765, a Parisian soup vendor named Boulanger gave to his soups the name, 'restaurants', that is, 'restoratives', and put up a sign, 'Boulanger vends les restaurants magiques'. To embellish his sign, he added a culinary joke in Latin: 'Venite ad me; vos qui stomacho laboratis, et ego restaurabo vos.' Encouraged by the success of his advertising, he augmented the menu by offering sheeps' feet in white sauce. Irate traiteurs brought a lawsuit against him to prevent his usurping their corporate rights. The lawsuit went in M. Boulanger's favour, and he became the first successful restauranteur.

The elevation of soup from rib-sticking stew to haute cuisine owed much to Carême and his predecessors. The influence of women was restricted as gastronomic occasions, particularly in England, were attended only by men until mid-Victorian days, when the food tended to be assessed largely for its quantity, the drink for its potency. It was not until the diverse arts of Escoffier and César Ritz combined exquisite taste in food and hotel architecture that women of fashion were persuaded to dine in public. This they did, in greater and greater numbers, as the Grande Cuisine of the great French chefs of the early 19th century filtered across the Channel and across the Atlantic. Great chefs created new dishes and named them after great ladies. Poires Mary Garden were consumed by men and women in fashionable restaurants; Consommé Princess Alice had pride of place on country house menus.

Not content merely to enjoy eating fine food, the ladies took to writing cookery books. In England, the Victorian housewife was regaled with advice on domestic cookery from Mrs. Beeton, and the more original Eliza Acton. Miss Acton's suggestion that wider use of the pot-au-feu would improve the diet of the poor has not been taken up, but her *Modern Cookery*, published in 1845, did much to influence contemporary cooks.

About soup, Eliza had this to say: 'Families who have resided much abroad, and those accustomed to continental modes of service, prefer it (soup) usually in any form to the more solid and heavy dishes which still often supersede it altogether at our tables, and which are so oppressive, not only to foreigners, but to all persons generally to whom circumstances have rendered them unaccustomed diet.'

Much has been written in praise of soup. Grimond de la Regnière eulogized, 'Soup is to a dinner what the porch or gateway is to a building'; Escoffier elaborated, 'that is to say, it must not only form the first portion thereof, but it must be so devised as to convey some idea of the whole to which it belongs; or, after the manner of an overture in a light opera, it should divulge what is to be the dominant phrase of the melody throughout.'

The Mock Turtle summed it up in two lines of doggerel:
'Who would not give all else for twop-
Ennyworth only of beautiful soup?'

CHAPTER ONE

Tools

THE MOST ELABORATE *batterie de cuisine* cannot turn an indifferent cook into a chef. But even an apprentice needs tools, and there are a few tools which seem to me essential to the making of soup on any reasonable scale.

My first essential is what the Americans call an electric blender, and what the English call an electric liquidizer. Get the largest one you can afford. It will liberate you. Some cookery experts say that a blender is less good for puréeing soup than the old way with sieves; some people would rather strike two sticks together than light a match. The blender is a blessing. Use it. But, use it safely. Never turn on the switch until the top is firmly on the container. Bad burns can ensue if the liquid in the container is hot and splashes. Never stir the contents in the container until the blender is turned off. Contact with the blades will either ruin your spoon, or the spoon will ruin the blades.

Another useful piece of soup-making equipment is a moulinette. The best sort has three removable discs for fine, medium and coarse purées.

Have a capacious mortar and pestle for pounding. Modern equipment has assumed many of its jobs, but there are still ingredients, like prawn shells and garlic and juniper berries and peppercorns, which can only be reduced to their proper consistency by old-fashioned mashing with a pestle. Also, a mortar has a pleasant shape, and can be filled with apples when not in use.

A drum sieve is a useful object, but it is best used with a pestle. A good assortment of sieves with different sized mesh will make life more pleasant in a soup kitchen, and conical sieves are excellent when making soups and sauces.

Pots, pans and casseroles should have heavy bottoms so that they sit correctly on the stove, and conduct heat in such a way that the contents do not stick or scorch. Stainless steel with a cast aluminium bottom is a good heat conductor. Copper pots are the most satisfactory to cook with if their bottoms are thick, and their handles of heavy iron. The pot is lined with a wash of tin, which must be renewed when it begins to wear off, that is, when the copper begins to show through. Copper is an excellent heat conductor, and the tin lining prevents discoloration of the food.

For soup-making, a cavernous soup pot is absolutely necessary. It may be made of earthenware, in which case you should protect it from burner heat with an asbestos mat. A new earthenware stock pot should have water boiled in it before it is used for stock or soup, and it should be washed in hot water only, without any soda or soap. A heavy French stew pan (marmite à ragoût) would be good for soup. Even better would be a large stock pot (grande marmite), but my best soup comes out of a simple black iron gypsy pot. This pot has a 6¾ litres capacity; it is of heavy iron construction and it has a tight-fitting tin top. It is the most satisfactory pot I have used for making soup, and it is large enough to hold large birds and half hams. It is also excellent for making stews and cassoulets, and it will hold a family-sized pot-au-feu. For the Lucullan Potée Normande (p. 73), you will need something bigger.

For chopping leeks and potatoes and oxtails, you need a large wooden chopping board. A really large one will save time and temper, and I really wouldn't bother with the small and arty ones shaped like an onion or an ear of corn.

For chopping bones or carcasses, a small cleaver is helpful. Kitchen scissors are useful for snipping cooked pasta or chives. The circular Swiss vegetable chopper with stainless steel blades and a spring handle is a wonderful mincer, particularly of onions, as it cuts down the flow of tears. A good potato peeler takes the anguish out of disrobing all sorts of vegetables. You should have at least three knives which can be made razor sharp, and a sharpening steel or simple knife sharpener to keep them that way. Plain carbon steel knives are best for this. They should be washed separately by hand after use, and tarnished blades should be cleaned with steel wool. They are worth the trouble, as they will chop or cut more quickly and efficiently than stainless steel, which is too hard to take a really good cutting edge.

You will need a bevy of over-sized spoons for soup: wooden spoons, slotted spoons, ladles, tasting spoons. For transatlantic cooks, it is useful to have a standard American measuring cup, and a nest of American measuring spoons with sizes of 1 tablespoon, 1 teaspoon, ½ teaspoon, ¼ teaspoon. For the English cook coping with metrication, a set of scales with both metric and imperial weights would be worth investing in, as would a metal cook's measure which contains millilitres, ounces and grams, as well as American and British cups and pints.

For transferring a large volume of puréed soup from blender back to soup pot, or for holding the liquid while you catch the bones in a sieve, you need several very large mixing bowls. Crockery ones are better than plastic, as plastic tends to cling to old odours. It also melts if placed too close to a burner or gas flame.

There are many other bits of equipment to elaborate the art of soup making. There are large or small Charlotte moulds for making royales, piping bags for quenelles, hors d'oeuvre cutters for cutting garnishes into fancy shapes, special bains-maries for cosseting delicate soups. If you are a collector of *batterie de cuisine* and have lots of storage space, the choice is infinite. But I have tried to limit this chapter to those tools without which the creation of an exquisite soup would be a morning's instead of an hour's work.

CHAPTER TWO

Some Notes On Stock

IT IS PERMISSABLE FOR MOST of the recipes in this book to use diluted stock cubes when 'stock' is a listed ingredient. Modern methods have produced these time-savers in an acceptable form, and they provide the foundation for many an honest and delicious soup.

An archetypal stock cube was used successfully in the 17th century on East Indian trading vessels. The meat was first roasted, then cut into small pieces and packed in a cask. Finally, melted butter was poured on to cover the meat and fill up the air spaces. These meat cubes were said to keep throughout a six months' voyage without developing taint.

Captain Cook took 'portable soup' with him on his voyage around the world in 1772. 'Portable soup' was made by evaporating clarified broth until it reached the consistency of glue. It could then be kept for many years, and it formed an important part of H.M. ships' stores until tinned meats came widely into favour about fifty years later.

In America, a form of stock cube was used as early as the mid-18th century in the Virginia Colony by travellers who stuffed their pockets with small patties of concentrated veal essence which could be dissolved in bowls of boiling water to make instant soup. When hot water was not available, they simply chewed these patties of pocket soup; paving the way, perhaps, for what has come to be called jellied consommé. Public acceptance of 'pocket soup' was assured when it finally achieved top place on the menu of one of Colonial Williamsburg's finest taverns, the Travis House, where it was listed in the company of such worthies as Southern Fried Chicken and Smoked Virginia Ham.

Stock cubes assuredly have their place in the soup kitchen, but should time be available, it is both pleasant and profitable to provide the foundation for soup from basic ingredients, and to make your own stock.

What is stock? The word has many meanings, not least of which is 'the liquor made by boiling bones or meat (with or without vegetables), and used as a foundation for soup.' Attributed to the mid-18th century, this definition evolved from other earlier ones, such as 'a fund or store'; 'a supporting structure'; 'the original from which something is derived'.

Translated into French, stock becomes 'fonds de cuisine', or the 'bottom', 'bed', 'substratum' of cooking. Much of the mystique which surrounds the making of stock may be attributed to the voluminous writings of the great French chefs of the last century. Consider, for example, the alarming list of ingredients proposed for a 'fonds simple' in Prosper Montagné's *Larousse Gastronomique*: 5 pounds lean beef, 5 pounds veal knuckle, 2 pounds fleshy beef and veal bones, ½ pound fresh bacon rind, ½ pound ham knuckle, with onions, carrots and garlic as aromatics.

As collectors' pieces, these old recipes are valuable additions to the kitchen shelf, but they are about as useful to the modern cook as grandma's antimacassar is to the modern housewife. Today, the construction of a good basic stock is easy, and the ingredients need not be expensive, but there are a few rules which sould be observed before setting out.

Vegetable parings and carcass bones can be used to make a small quantity of stock, as can meat trimmings or leftovers. But for a really clear stock, you must use raw bones. Cooked bones can be combined with raw bones if the stock is to be used on the same day, but stock made exclusively from raw bones keeps better and provides more flavour. Long and slow simmering is essential, as hard boiling will produce muddy stock. Raw lamb bones and turnips are best left out of stocks, except in making Scotch Broth, as their strong flavour could spoil the taste of the soup. Chicken giblets are ideal for making stock, but exclude the liver, which imparts a bitter flavour, and is better saved for making pâtés or sauce for spaghetti. If you are making stock from leftovers, use the following method: place the meat or chicken trimmings, giblets, bacon rinds or a ham or bacon bone in a large saucepan. Add a plateful of cut-up vegetables, a bouquet garni, a few peppercorns, and pour on cold water to cover the ingredients by two-thirds. Salt very lightly, or not at all if there is a ham or bacon bone in the pot. Bring slowly to the boil, skim, half-cover the pan, and simmer 1½ to 2 hours. The liquid should be reduced by a third. Strain, and when the stock is cold, skim to remove the fat. For a stronger stock, use raw bones and proceed according to the following recipes.

Brown Stock

1¼ kg (3 lb) beef bones	bouquet garni
(or mixed beef and veal)	6 peppercorns
2 quartered onions	salt
2 quartered carrots	water
1 sliced stick celery	

Wipe the bones, but do not wash them. Put into a 6¾-litre

(12 pint) saucepan, and set on low heat. Leave to fry gently
for 15–20 minutes. Add no fat unless the bones are very dry,
as there should be sufficient in the bone marrow. After 10
minutes, add the vegetables. When bones and vegetables
are lightly coloured, add the herbs, peppercorns and water
to cover up to two thirds the ingredients. Salt sparingly, as
the stock may otherwise become too salty in the process of
reduction. Bring slowly to the boil, skimming; half cover the
pan and simmer for 4–5 hours, or until a good flavour is
obtained. Strain and use for brown sauces, casseroles, or in
recipes calling for jellied stock. The bones may be boiled up
again, and while the resulting stock will be weaker, it is
useful for soups and gravies.

White Stock

1¼ kg (*3 lb*) *veal bones*	*bouquet garni*
2 quartered onions	*6 peppercorns*
2 quartered carrots	*salt*
1 stick sliced celery	*water*

Wipe, do not wash, the bones. Put into a 6¾ litre (12 pint)
saucepan, add water to cover by two thirds, and bring to the
boil, slowly, skimming. When well skimmed and bubbling,
add the vegetables, herbs, peppercorns and a very little salt
and seasoning. Half cover the pan, and simmer as for
Brown Stock.

Vegetable Stock

450 g (1 lb) carrots	*3–4 peppercorns*
450 g (1 lb) onions	*1 teaspoon tomato purée*
½ head celery	*salt*
15 g (½ oz) butter	*water*

Quarter the vegetables, and brown lightly in a large saucepan. Add peppercorns, tomato purée, water to cover, and
salt. Bring to the boil, cover, and simmer for 2 hours, or
until well flavoured.

Chicken Stock

For chicken, you may substitute any poultry or game; the method is the same.

*chicken giblets (excluding the   salt
    liver), bones and trimmings   5 peppercorns
1 onion   1⅛ litres (2 pints) cold water
bouquet garni*

Wash but do not peel the onion, and cut in half. Dry fry the giblets, raw bones and trimmings with the onion, using barely enough fat to cover the bottom of the pan, and allow the pan to get very hot before putting in the onion and giblets. Cook on full heat until lightly coloured. Remove from the heat, and add the water, a big pinch of salt, the peppercorns, a light seasoning of salt and bouquet garni. (If using cooked bones and trimmings, add them at this point.) Simmer gently, covered, for 1–2 hours.

FISH STOCK

Fishmongers will often give away the trimmings needed to make fish stock. If you do have to pay, the sum will be small. Ask for turbot and sole bones, as their gelatine content is high, and the resulting stock will have a good texture.

*1–1¼ kg (2¼–3 lb) fish   10 peppercorns
    trimmings (bones, skin,   1 dessertspoon white wine
    head, etc.)   vinegar
1 large sliced onion   140–280 ml (¼–½ pint) dry
1 medium sliced carrot   white wine
5 cm (2 in) piece celery   water
white part of 1 leek*

Note: If you have no wine, substitute an extra tablespoon of white wine vinegar, and 2 or 3 lumps sugar.

Put the fish trimmings into a large soup kettle. Add the other ingredients with water to cover. Salt should be added later, after the stock has been reduced, or the process of reduction may produce a stock which is too salty. Bring to the boil, skim well, and simmer, covered, for $\frac{1}{2}$ hour. Strain through a muslin-lined sieve before reducing to the desired consistency; overboiling of fish bones produces gluey stock.

A Note on Storage

Stock may either be stored in a refrigerator or deep frozen. First, remove every speck of fat in one of the following ways. Let the stock settle for about 5 minutes, remove the fat from the surface with a ladle, then draw pieces of absorbent paper across the surface to collect any remaining bits of grease. Or, you may place the cooled stock, uncovered, in the refrigerator until the fat has hardened on the surface, when it can be scraped off.

When degreased and quite cold, cover the stock and refrigerate or deep freeze. Refrigerated stock should not be stored for more than 24 hours without re-boiling, as it can easily spoil. To freeze, put stock in a strong plastic container with a lid, or in one of the cartons available at most frozen food centres especially designed for freezing liquids. When a small amount of very concentrated stock is needed for a soup or sauce, the stock may be frozen in ice cube trays, covered with freezer wrap. Frozen stock may be used straight from the freezer, but heat it slowly at first to ensure that it blends properly with other ingredients.

CHAPTER THREE

Fish and Shellfish Soups

EARLY ENGLISH COOKERY BOOKS ARE full of recipes for freshwater fish for the very good reason that transport of sea fish to inland towns was slow, and the transport of fresh fish over any distance was impracticable. In the 16th century, most of the fish landed at London's water gate was salted or pickled, unless it came to the fish market from the nearby Essex or Kentish coasts. Fresh fish was brought to London from the rivers, brooks and ponds of the surrounding country, although old records contain the information that 'a great store of very good fish of diuers sortes' could be found in the 'towne ditch' outside the city walls. The ancient Fishmongers' Company, which was incorporated in 1536, brought together the Stockfishmongers, who dealt in dried fish, mainly from Iceland and Norway, and the Saltfishmongers, who handled the large quantities of salted and pickled herrings, cod, eels, whiting and mackerel brought from the East Coast, Holland and the Baltic.

Contrary to general belief 'fysshe dayes' were imposed on

the people by the Church, not so much for religious principles of abstinence, but to compensate for the dearth of good meat, and to fortify the navy. According to William Harrison, writing in his *Description of England* in 1557, 'fysshe dayes' were introduced not for 'religious sake or publike order,' but 'to the end our numbers of cattell may be the better increased, and that abundance of fish which the sea yeeldeth, more generallie receiued. Beside this, there is the great consideration had in making of this law for the preseruation of the nauie, and maintenance of conuenient numbers of sea faring men, both which would otherwise greatlie decaie, if some means were not found whereby they might be increased.' Indeed, by 1563, the eating of fish was deemed so important that an Act was passed to enforce the observance of two fish days a week, with an accompanying fine for non-observance to the sum of £3, or 'three months close imprisonment'.

English cooks seem to have come late to the talent of combining the fruits of their seas in recipes for soup, perhaps because of an attitude of mind expressed by the colloquialism 'a pretty kettle of fish'. Early seafood stews were concocted from oysters and mussels, once so cheap and abundant that vendors cried their wares on every London street. Crayfish were used to enliven the dull appearance of bisques previously made only of meat and breadcrumbs.

French chefs were more imaginative, turning Mediterranean fishes into concoctions such as the famed Bouillabaisse, whose praises have been sung both in verse and prose. Bouillabaisse is said to have connections with Roman gastronomy, but contemporary versions are based on a recipe published by Prosper Merimée in 1840. Unfortunately, a genuine Marseille Bouillabaisse can only be made with the rascasse, or spiny scorpion fish, as a prime ingredient, but a recipe for it is included in this chapter for the sake of those who yearn for the odours and flavours of Riviera ports.

African Fish Soup

1 large white fish
2 onions
1 bay leaf
1 clove
1 tablespoon tomato purée
2 potatoes, peeled and diced
2 carrots, peeled and diced

1 tablespoon curry powder
2 tablespoons oil
2 teaspoons lemon juice
salt and pepper
4 tablespoons cream, or ailloli
  (see p. 62)

Fillet the fish. Put the bones and head into 1 litre (1¾ pints) cold water. Add 1 peeled onion, bay leaf, clove, salt and pepper. Bring to the boil and simmer for 1 hour. Strain, keeping the liquid. Chop the second onion and fry in oil until golden. Add curry powder, mixing well. Combine with fish stock, tomato purée, potatoes and carrots, and cook until vegetables are just tender. While the soup is cooking, place a metal colander over the saucepan and in it steam the fish fillets. This will not take long. When tender, flake the fish, and just before serving, add it to the soup together with the lemon juice and cream. If using ailloli instead of cream, serve it separately.

Jerusalem Artichoke and Scallop Soup

1 kg (2¼ lb) Jerusalem
  artichokes
2 scallops
2 medium onions

1 litre (1¾ pints) white stock
60 g (2 oz) butter
1 tablespoon flour
salt and pepper

Clean the scallops and cut the white part into thin slices, and the roe into two or three pieces. Cover with equal parts of milk and water, add 4 peppercorns and a pinch of salt, and simmer for 10 minutes. Peel the artichokes and the onions and slice them into a large soup pan in which you have melted the butter. Soften in the butter for a few minutes, but do not brown. Sprinkle on the flour and stir in thoroughly, then add the stock. Simmer for about 30 minutes until the artichokes are tender. Sieve, blend or mouli the mixture, and return to the washed pan. Add the scallops and their cooking liquid. Stir and bring to boiling point, adding a little cream to serve.

BISQUE

Now used to describe a purée, particularly of shellfish served as a thick soup, a bisque was originally a soup made from some sort of meat and breadcrumbs. In the 18th century, bisque soups were concoctions of boiled poultry and game, sometimes served with a garnish of cockscombs, and usually very highly spiced. According to E. Darenne, writing on bisques in *La Cuisine Française*, the first link with modern bisques appeared in the last edition of *Dons de Comus* in 1758, with a recipe for quail soup with crayfish. This was a bisque soup (contained bread boiled to a pulp) made of quails with a topping of crayfish purée. Also included was a recipe for a bisque soup made of pigeons and crayfish. The crayfish was probably introduced to give a rosy colour to the soup.

Crab Bisque

1 cooked crab
1 litre (1¾ pints) fish stock
handful of rice
1 small onion
few parsley stalks

1 bay leaf
15 g (½ oz) butter
teaspoonful of brandy
cream

Carefully pick the meat from the crab, reserving the white flesh from the claws. Pound the rest in a mortar, and simmer with the rice, chopped onion, parsley stalks and bay leaf in the fish fumet for ½ hour. Remove the bay leaf and the parsley stalks, and either sieve or blend. Heat very gently with the butter, brandy and a little cream. At the last minute add the flesh from the claws, flaked finely.

Bisque d'Écrevisses

1 small carrot
1 small onion
2 stalks parsley
100 g (3½ oz) butter
thyme
1 bay leaf
560 g (1¼ lb) crayfish

2 tablespoons brandy
140 ml (¼ pint) white wine
1¼ litres (2½ pints) white stock
85 g (3 oz) rice
3 tablespoons double cream
salt and pepper
cayenne

Dice the carrot and peeled onion, and chop the parsley. Add a pinch of thyme and the bay leaf, and lightly brown this mirepoix in 30 g (1 oz) butter. Add the crayfish, which should be very small ones, and toss them in the mixture until they turn bright red. Sprinkle with the brandy, which should first be flamed, add the white wine, season with salt and pepper, and reduce slightly. Moisten with 140 ml (¼ pint) stock, and cook gently for 10 minutes. Cook the rice in 1 litre (1¾ pints) of the stock. Drain the crayfish of all cooking liquor, reserving the tails for garnish. Pound them in a mortar with the mirepoix. Add the cooked rice and the cooking liquor, and sieve, then mouli or blend. Add 280 ml (½ pint) stock to the purée, and bring to the boil, whisking. Finish with 70 g (2½ oz) butter and the cream and a pinch of cayenne. Garnish with the shelled crayfish tails.

Lobster Bisque

2 medium boiled lobsters
560 ml (1 pint) white stock
1 onion
4 ribs celery with leaves
2 whole cloves
1 bay leaf
6 peppercorns
60 g (2 oz) butter

60 g (2 oz) flour
¾ litre (1¼ pints) milk
salt
¼ teaspoon nutmeg
140 ml (¼ pint) cream
parsley
paprika

Remove the meat from the body and claws of the lobsters, discarding the sac behind the head and the intestinal vein. Dice the meat, and reserve. If there is coral, reserve this also. Crack the shells and combine them with the stock, sliced onion, celery, cloves, bay leaf, peppercorns. Simmer these for ½ hour, then strain. Melt the butter in the washed pan. Stir in the flour, and gradually add the hot milk. Season with 1 teaspoon salt and the nutmeg. If you have lobster coral, force it through a sieve and combine it with the butter before adding the flour and the milk. When the sauce is smooth and boiling, add the lobster meat and the strained stock. Simmer the bisque very gently, covered, for 5 minutes. Remove from heat and stir in the scalded cream. Serve at once with a sprinkling of parsley and paprika.

Oyster Bisque

560 ml (1 pint) oysters	*140 ml (¼ pint) cream*
30 g (1 oz) butter	*2 egg yolks*
1 tablespoon grated onion	*parsley*
22½ g (¾ oz) flour	*salt*
560 ml (1 pint) milk	*paprika or cayenne*

Heat but do not boil the oysters. Drain them, reserving the liquor, and put them through a meat grinder or chop them finely. Melt the butter in a heavy pan and lightly sauté the grated onion; add the flour and stir until smooth. Add the oyster liquor, milk, cream, ½ teaspoon salt, and ½ teaspoon paprika or a good pinch of cayenne. Stir until smooth and boiling, then add the oysters. Remove the bisque from the fire. Combine and beat the yolks and 2 tablespoons water. Add a little hot bisque to this mixture, then add the mixture slowly to the hot bisque, stirring. Stir the bisque over a very low flame for 1 minute, or place it over hot water until ready to serve. On no account allow it to boil. Just before serving, sprinkle with chopped parsley.

Salmon Bisque

½ clove garlic
1 small onion, sliced
½ green pepper, chopped
15 g (½ oz) butter
225 g (8 oz) tinned salmon
2 tablespoons dry sherry
280 ml (½ pint) milk

¼ teaspoon Tabasco sauce
30 g (1 oz) dill weed
1 teaspoon salt
¼ teaspoon pepper
140 ml (¼ pint) double or
    whipping cream

Sauté the garlic, onion and pepper in the butter. In an electric blender, purée the sautéed vegetables and remaining ingredients except the cream. Cover, and blend on high speed 15 seconds, or until smooth. Turn to low speed and pour in the cream. Serve hot, or chilled.

Seafood Bisque

450 g (1 lb) tomatoes
2 onions
1⅛ litres (2 pints) water
1 teaspoon lemon juice
salt and pepper
450 g (1 lb) white fish

140 ml (¼ pint) single cream
2 tablespoons dill, finely
    chopped
60–110 g (2–4 oz) peeled
    prawns

Peel and chop tomatoes and onions. Combine with water and lemon juice in a saucepan, season with salt and pepper, bring to the boil and simmer 20 minutes. Cut fish into cubes and add to soup, cooking until fish is barely tender. Stir in cream, check seasoning, add dill and prawns, and reheat gently.

La Bouillabaisse

For ten people:

2 kg (4½ lb) fresh fish,
    which must include rascasse,
    and an assortment of at least
    some of the following:
    angler fish, weaver fish,
    John Dory, sea-hen,
    whiting and crayfish, trimmed
    and cut into neat pieces
2 onions, chopped

4 tomatoes, chopped
4 garlic cloves, chopped
3 tablespoons olive oil
2 sprigs fennel
a good pinch powdered saffron
a bay leaf
15 g (½ oz) sea salt
7 g (¼ oz) pepper
1 loaf French bread

In a large, heavy, wide cooking pot put the onions, tomatoes and garlic. Moisten with the olive oil, and add the fennel, bay leaf and saffron. Season with salt and pepper. Mix together and add the firm fish; add soft fish such as John Dory, sea-hen and whiting 5 minutes later. Pour over boiling water to cover. Put the pan over high heat, and boil the mixture rapidly for 12 to 15 minutes. Cut the French bread into slices and dry them in the oven. When the soup is ready, arrange the fish slices on a platter to serve separately with the soup. Put the bread in a deep dish and pour the sieved soup over it. Sprinkle parsley on top and serve immediately.

Catherine's Fish Soup

1 red snapper (which can be
    bought frozen from speciality
    fishmongers)
1 big onion
10 cloves of garlic
2 big potatoes
croûtons
olive oil

4 tomatoes
sprig of rosemary
1 teaspoon chopped marjoram
1 carrot
celery leaves
2 bay leaves
Parmesan cheese

Fry chopped onions in oil, then add the whole garlic cloves, peeled. Slice the potatoes, and add to the onions, frying for a few minutes. Then add the fish (head and all), rosemary, marjoram, bay leaves, tomatoes quartered, celery leaves and sliced carrot. Cover with water, season with salt and pepper, and boil gently for approximately 15 minutes. Put all but the fish through a medium sieve. Reserve the flesh of the fish, discarding head and bones, and add to the soup. Simmer all together for about 5 minutes. Float garlic croûtons on top of the soup, and cover with *rouille*; then sprinkle Parmesan cheese on top.

Rouille: make mayonnaise with 2 yolks and olive oil. Add 1 pounded clove of garlic, and paprika or saffron to colour.

Clam Chowder

1 large onion
15 g (½ oz) butter
280 ml (½ pint) white stock
3 medium potatoes

560 ml (1 pint) milk
1 tin (285 g/10 oz) baby clams
60 g (2 oz) grated cheese
chopped parsley

Slice a large onion, and sweat until tender, but do not brown, in the butter. Add hot stock and diced potatoes. Add seasoning, and cover and simmer gently for 15 minutes, or until potatoes are tender. Sieve or blend, return to clean pan, and add milk and the clams. Again bring to the boil, stir in grated cheese and chopped parsley.

New England Clam Chowder

You will have to use tinned clams if you live away from those parts of the world where clams are abundant.

1⅛ litres (2 pints) shucked
* clams, or 2 285-g (10-oz)*
* tins baby clams*
110 g (4 oz) salt pork or 3
* rashers streaky bacon*
1 large onion

3 tablespoons flour
4 medium sized potatoes, diced
45 g (1½ oz) butter
1 litre (1¾ pints) milk
salt and pepper
pilot biscuits or oyster crackers

Wash the clams in ¾ litre (1¼ pints) water. Drain, reserving the water. Sieve the liquid. If using hard-shelled clams, cut the hard part away from the soft part. Chop finely the hard part of the clams, the bacon or pork, and the onion. Sauté the pork slowly in a nut of butter. Remove and reserve the scraps. Add the minced onion and hard part of the clams to the fat. Stir and cook slowly for 5 minutes. Sift the flour over them and stir until blended. Heat and stir in the reserved clam liquid. Peel and cut the potatoes into 1 cm (½ in) dice, and add to the mixture. Cover the pan and simmer until the potatoes are done but still firm. Add the pork scraps, the soft part of the clams, and the butter. Simmer for about 3 minutes. Heat the milk to boiling point. Place the chowder in a heated tureen, and pour the hot milk over it. Season with salt and freshly ground black pepper to taste, and serve, accompanied by pilot biscuits or oyster crackers.

Note: if using tinned clams, strain the juice and add water to make up to scant ¾ litre (1¼ pints) liquid. Use this liquid in place of the water measurement given. Omit all references to the hard part of the mollusc.

Cod Fish Soup

450 g (1 lb) filleted cod
2 leeks
2 medium potatoes
1 celery stalk
¼ teaspoon mixed spice (nutmeg pepper, allspice, clove)

30 g (1 oz) butter
1⅛ litres (2 pints) water or fish stock
salt
chopped dill, parsley or chives

Clean the leeks thoroughly, removing the green tops, and cut the white part into thin slices. Peel the potatoes, and cut into small dice. Cut the celery into small dice. Melt the butter in a soup pan. Add the vegetables, and fry gently until the leeks are soft and transparent, but do not allow them to brown. Add the mixed spice, and pour over the stock or water. Season with salt. Bring to the boil, and cook gently for 10 minutes. Cut the fish into small dice, and add to the soup. Continue to cook very gently for a further 10 minutes, or until the vegetables are tender. Sprinkle with chopped dill, parsley or chives before serving.

Crab Soup

225 g (8 oz) tinned or cooked
   crab meat
4 tablespoons chopped spring
   onions
2 tablespoons olive oil
1¾ litres (3 pints) white stock

2 egg whites
2 tablespoons cooked ham
½ teaspoon ground ginger
2 tablespoons sherry
salt and pepper

Brown crab meat and onions in hot oil in a saucepan over high heat for a minute or two. Add seasonings and stock. Bring to the boil. Add slightly beaten egg whites slowly, stirring constantly for about 1 minute. Serve with a sprinkling of minced ham.

Crab Gumbo

2 rashers bacon
15 g (½ oz) butter
400 g (14 oz) tin or 450 g
   (1 lb) fresh okra (ladies'
   fingers)
1 onion
400 g (14 oz) tin tomatoes
1 tablespoon flour

1 clove garlic
½ lemon
1 bay leaf
225 g (8 oz) fresh or tinned
   crab meat
salt
paprika

Sauté the minced bacon lightly in the butter. Add the sliced okra (if using fresh okra) and the chopped onion, and brown lightly. Add the tomatoes, crushed and minced garlic, sliced lemon, and bay leaf. Bring these ingredients to the boil, then add 1⅛ litres (2 pints) boiling water or stock, a pinch of salt, and a pinch of paprika. Simmer gently for 45 minutes, covered. Combine the flour with 2 tablespoons water. Stir into it a little hot soup, then add the paste to the soup. (If using tinned okra, add at this point, straining off the juices). Add the crab meat and adjust the seasoning. Make very hot, and serve at once. Accompany with steamed rice, if you want to turn the gumbo into a main course.

Okra is a member of the mallow family, prolific in South America and the Southern states of America, in West Africa and India, where it is cultivated and eaten as a vegetable. The young pods tapering to slender points bear a strong resemblance to the ladies' fingers whose name they also bear.

Creole Shrimp Gumbo

450 g (1 lb) gammon
1 kg (2¼ lb) okra (ladies' fingers), or 2 (400-g/14-oz) tins
4 medium onions
2 ribs celery with leaves
½ green pepper

2 cloves garlic
1 sprig thyme
1 bay leaf
5 tomatoes
450 g (1 lb) shrimps or prawns
parsley

Sauté the gammon lightly in a little fat, then cut it into dice. In the dripping, sauté the okra, cut into 1 cm (½ in) slices. (If using tinned okra, add 5 minutes before the end of cooking time.) Add and briefly sauté the onions, finely chopped. Add the chopped celery, the chopped green pepper, the crushed and minced garlic, the thyme, the bay leaf, the peeled and seeded tomatoes, and 1¼ litres (2½ pints) water. Shell and remove veins from the shrimp or prawns. Bring the mixture to the boil, then reduce heat, and add the ham, shrimp or prawns, and 2 tablespoons chopped parsley. Simmer very gently for ½ hour. (Tinned okra should be added at this point. Bring the mixture back to boiling point, simmer for 5 minutes more very gently.) Serve. Gumbo may be served as a main dish with steamed or boiled rice. Use less water to produce a thicker gumbo.

Cullen Skink (Smoked Haddock Soup)

675 g (1½ lb) smoked haddock
fillets
1 onion
¾ litre (1¼ pints) milk
225 g (½ lb) cooked potatoes,
mashed

2 bay leaves
salt
pinch nutmeg
white pepper
140 ml (¼ pint) single cream
1 tablespoon chopped parsley

Peel and thinly slice onion and divide into rings. Place haddock fillets in a lightly greased baking dish, top with onion rings, and pour over just enough water to cover. Cover with foil and bake in moderate oven (350°F or Reg. 4) for about 20 minutes or until fish is just tender. Drain off and reserve the liquid and discard the onion. Remove skin from fish and carefully flake the flesh. Combine milk in saucepan with potatoes, and heat, stirring continually until mixture comes to the boil and is creamy smooth. Add bay leaves and the fish cooking liquid, and simmer for 5 minutes. Remove bay leaves, add fish, season with salt, pepper and a little ground nutmeg. Add cream and heat through. Sprinkle with chopped parsley before serving.

Curried Fish Soup

1 kg (2¼ lb) white fish
30 g (1 oz) butter
1 Spanish onion, sliced
1 carrot, sliced
1 turnip, sliced
1 tablespoon curry powder
2 tablespoons flour

1¾ litres (3 pints) well-
flavoured fish stock
salt and freshly ground black
pepper
140 ml (¼ pint) double cream
lemon juice

Wash the fish and cut it into small pieces. Melt the butter in a saucepan, add sliced vegetables and sauté them until blended. Stir in the curry powder. Add fish and fish stock, and stir until boiling. Season with salt and pepper, lower heat, and simmer gently for 10 minutes. Lift out the best pieces of fish, and reserve them to serve in the soup. Simmer soup for $1\frac{1}{2}$ hours more, skimming if necessary. Strain soup through a fine sieve, rubbing through a little of the fish and vegetables without allowing any bones to pass through. Reheat soup in a clean saucepan; add cream and cooked fish, and lemon juice to taste.

Dutch Eel Soup

*large eel (675 g / $1\frac{1}{2}$ lb), cut in
  short lengths
18 peppercorns
2 heaped teaspoons salt
bouquet garni
85 g (3 oz) butter*

*60 g (2 oz) flour
2 egg yolks
2 tablespoons double cream
lemon juice, salt, pepper
chopped parsley
croûtons*

Combine eel, peppercorns, salt and bouquet garni in a pan, cover with water, and bring to the boil. Simmer gently for about 15 minutes, or until the eel can be removed from its bones. Remove eel and discard bones. Mash 60 g (2 oz) butter and the flour, and add to the simmering stock in small pieces to thicken, then leave for 10 minutes. Beat yolks and cream together, pour in a little soup, return to the pan together with the eel, and stir for 5 minutes without allowing it to come near the boiling point. Taste and season with lemon juice, adding more salt and pepper, if necessary. Remove the bouquet. Whisk in the remaining butter; add parsley, and serve with croûtons.

Lettuce Fish Soup

*225 g (8 oz) fillet of white fish
$\frac{1}{2}$ head lettuce
$1\frac{1}{4}$ litres ($2\frac{1}{2}$ pints) water
$\frac{1}{2}$ teaspoon cornflour
1 tablespoon salad oil
$\frac{1}{4}$ teaspoon sugar*

*2 tablespoons soy sauce
$\frac{1}{2}$ teaspoon ground ginger
$\frac{1}{4}$ teaspoon pepper
1 teaspoon monosodium
  glutamate (optional)
salt*

Slice the fish thinly, and mix it with the cornflour, oil, seasonings. Let stand for 10 minutes. Bring water to the boil in a soup pan, stir in shredded lettuce, cover, and simmer for 2 to 3 minutes. Stir in seasoned fish slices, and simmer for 3 to 5 minutes. Serve very hot.

Mussel Soup

1⅛ litres (2 pints) mussels	*22½ g (¾ oz) flour*
450 g (1 lb) fish bones	*60 g (2 oz) butter*
210 ml (1½ gills) white wine	*70 ml (½ gill) cream*
slice of onion	*1 egg yolk*
¾ litre (1¼ pints) water	*chopped parsley*
bouquet garni	*2 slices stale bread*
clove of garlic	*salt and pepper*

Put the fish bones into a pan with half the wine and all the water. Add the herbs and garlic. Bring to the boil, and simmer for 20 minutes. Melt in a pan 30 g (1 oz) of butter. Off the fire, add the flour and seasoning. Stir until smooth. Strain on the fish stock and bring to the boil. Simmer for 15 minutes. Wash and scrub the mussels, discarding any open ones. Put into a pan with the rest of the wine. Cover and bring quickly to the boil. Shake over the heat for 2 or 3 minutes. Strain the liquor into the soup. Shell the mussels and remove beards. Add the mussels to the soup, and barely simmer for 5 minutes. Add remaining butter. Mix the yolks and the cream, and pour into the soup off the heat. Heat again, but do not boil. Float croûtons of fried bread on top.

Potage Crème de Crevettes

2 small carrots	*70 ml (½ gill) white wine*
110 g (4 oz) diced onions	*1 tablespoon brandy*
60 g (2 oz) diced celery	*1 tablespoon flour*
60 g (2 oz) butter	*1 litre (1¾ pints) milk*
340 g (12 oz) prawns or shrimps	*scant 280 ml (½ pint) cream*

Cook a mirepoix of the carrots, onions, and celery, all very finely chopped, in half the butter very slowly, until the vegetables are tender. Add to this the peeled prawns and sauté together for 2 minutes. Season with salt and pepper, and moisten with white wine and brandy, which has first been set alight. Cook together for 5 minutes, very gently. Reserve 12 prawn tails for garnish, and blend the mixture, or pound it in a mortar. Make a Béchamel sauce with the remainder of the butter, the flour, and the milk. Add the shrimp mixture to this, and mouli or blend. Reheat, taste for seasoning, and finish with the cream. Garnish with the prawn tails.

Prawn Chowder

60 g (2 oz) butter	*1 bay leaf*
2 stalks celery	*salt and pepper*
1 onion	*paprika*
½ green pepper	*225 g (8 oz) peeled prawns*
840 ml (1½ pints) chicken stock	*1 small packet frozen peas*
1 small tin tomatoes	*(225 g/8 oz)*
(225 g/8 oz)	

Chop the celery finely. Peel and chop the onion. Seed, core and chop the pepper. Melt the butter in a saucepan. Add the celery, onion and pepper, and cook over medium heat until the onion is transparent. Add the chicken stock, tomatoes, and the bay leaf. Season with salt, pepper and paprika. Cover and simmer gently for 20 minutes. Add the prawns and peas. Mix well. Cook for a further 10 minutes, barely simmering.

Scallop Soup

6 small scallops
1 small onion
60 g (2 oz) butter
45 g (1½ oz) flour
560 ml (1 pint) milk
2 tablespoons cream

280 ml (½ pint) fish or chicken
  stock
2 tablespoons chopped parsley
salt and pepper
1 tablespoon dry vermouth

Remove the thin black line of intestine from the scallops. Chop the white part. Leave the coral whole. Peel and finely chop the onion. Melt the butter in a saucepan. Add the scallops and chopped onions. Cook over medium heat until the onions are soft, about 5 minutes. Add the flour and mix well. Gradually add the milk, stirring constantly until the sauce is thick and smooth. Add the stock, and bring back to the boil. Cook for 5 minutes over medium heat. Remove the soup from the heat, stir in the cream and the chopped parsley. Season with salt and pepper and a little dry vermouth. Serve hot with garlic bread.

Zuppa di Pesce

1¼ kg (3 lb) fish : sole,
  mullet, mackerel, whiting
1 small eel
2 small squid
1 large onion
1 kg (2¼ lb) tomatoes
salt and pepper

2 tablespoons tomato paste
1 clove garlic
4 tablespoons chopped parsley
30 g (1 oz) butter
6 tablespoons olive oil
140 ml (¼ pint) dry white wine
1 tablespoon wine vinegar

Sauté the sliced onion in oil and butter until soft but not brown. Add peeled, seeded and diced tomatoes, tomato paste diluted with 140 ml (¼ pint) water, garlic and parsley. Simmer uncovered for 15 to 20 minutes. Add fish, cleaned and cut into big cubes, and enough boiling water to cover. Return to the boil, and add white wine and vinegar. Simmer gently for 15 minutes. Season to taste. Serve with garlic flavoured French bread.

CHAPTER FOUR

Poultry and Game Soups

POULTRY HAS BEEN A STAPLE of the English diet since medieval times, when every lord of the manor kept chickens and ducks, albeit as poor relations to his oxen, cows, sheep and pigs. The winter feeding of livestock was little understood, so it was customary to slaughter farm animals in late autumn. Chickens were able to survive on chaff and dried beans, and for that reason were widely used to supplement meagre diets throughout the winter months. Pigeon lofts and dovecotes were prominent features of most big estates, providing a reliable source of fresh meat throughout the year. The trapping and snaring of wild birds was carried out on a grand scale, not only by wealthy landowners, but also by villagers whose defiance of the laws against poaching was legion.

Ubiquitous as it was, poultry was not much esteemed until the 17th century, when it came to be regarded as something of a delicacy, and a climb up the class structure was assumed for those who could afford to buy a goose or a fine fat hen for their table. At that time, geese cost a colossal 3s, and the price of chickens had risen to 1s 4d, as compared with the mere 2d they were fetching a century before.

The Englishman's taste for domestic and wild birds has undergone many changes of fashion. We no longer eat swans and peacocks, although they were considered prime delicacies at every important banquet from Roman times up to the 16th century. Linnets and thrushes are no longer featured on menus, as they were before official action was taken to protect wild birds. A pie of live blackbirds would not be considered a dainty dish today, nor even a respectable culinary joke. The nursery rhyme is nonetheless based on truth: live birds actually flew out of pies in the 18th century; frogs even hopped from pastry cases to enliven the dinner parties of the idle rich.

Such frivolities would be frowned on by the French, who have traditionally been more serious about food. Chickens have long been highly favoured in France, and it is quite probable that the popularity of Henry IV owed less to his military prowess than to his expressed desire that every Frenchman should have a chicken for his cooking pot.

Modern methods of chicken farming have done little to improve the culinary status of poultry, but fortunately even tasteless battery birds can be transformed into tasty dishes through the alchemy which takes place in a good cook's soup pot.

African Chicken Soup

1 old hen
1 litre (1¾ pints) chicken stock
2 carrots, scraped and sliced
2 stalks celery, cut into pieces
1 onion stuck with a clove
1 bay leaf

4 potatoes
salt and pepper
40 ml (¼ pint) cream
juice of 1 lemon
1 egg
1 tablespoon flour

Bring the stock to the boil, together with carrots, celery and onion. Add chicken, season with salt and pepper, and simmer until chicken is tender. Strain and return the liquid to the pan. Add quartered potatoes, and cook until done. Meanwhile, remove the flesh from the chicken and cut into small pieces. Add the chicken and vegetables to the pan, heat, and just before serving, add cream mixed with flour, beaten egg and lemon juice. Heat again, but do not boil.

Bird's Nest Soup

85 g (3 oz) bird's nest
1¾ litres (3 pints) white stock
2 tablespoons uncooked ham
salt

225 g (8 oz) uncooked chicken
  breast
1 teaspoon monosodium
  glutamate (optional)

Soak bird's nest in warm water for 1 hour, or until water is absorbed. (Bird's nest is available from Chinese grocery or speciality shops.) Wash in fresh water and drain. Add drained nest to boiling white stock in soup pan. Add seasonings, cover, and simmer for 40 minutes. Add minced ham and chicken. Stir. Cover, and cook for 15 minutes.

Chicken Giblet Soup with Liver Dumplings

225 g (8 oz) chicken livers
450 g (1 lb) chicken giblets
2 chicken legs
100 g (3½ oz) butter
110 g (4 oz) flour plus
  1 tablespoon

1 large carrot
1 parsnip
salt and pepper
1 tablespoon parsley
1 egg
2 tablespoons soured cream

Put giblets in 1⅛ litres (2 pints) salted cold water, and bring to the boil, skimming. Reduce heat and simmer gently for 1 hour. Finely chop the carrot and parsnip. Melt 85 g (3 oz) butter in a heavy saucepan and add the vegetables. Sprinkle with salt and pepper, and cook gently, covered, for 15 minutes, shaking the pan occasionally. Add 1 tablespoon flour. Blend well, then add the water in which the giblets have cooked, straining off the giblets. Mince giblets and add to the soup. Bring to the boil, then lower heat to simmer. Put the remainder of the flour (generous measure) into a bowl. Beat the egg with a little water, and stir into the flour. Add about 140 ml (¼ pint) water, until you have a fairly thick dough. Chop the chicken livers very small and fry for 3 minutes in 15 g (½ oz) butter. Season. Add to the dough, blending well. Heat the soup to bubbling, then push teaspoonfuls of dough into it. Boil very gently for 3 or 4 minutes. By then, the dumplings should be swimming at the top of the soup. Remove soup from heat, and add the chopped parsley and soured cream.

Chicken Gumbo

1 boiling fowl
3 rashers streaky bacon
6 tomatoes
1 small tin whole corn kernels
  (326 g/11½ oz)
1 onion

225 g (8 oz) okra (ladies'
  fingers) or 1 340 g (12 oz)
  tin
60 g (2 oz) rice
salt
paprika

Joint the chicken and dredge with flour. Melt the chopped bacon in a large soup pan with a tablespoon of oil. Brown the chicken in the fat. Pour over it 1⅛ litres (2 pints) boiling water, and simmer covered until the chicken is very tender. This may take 2 hours or more, depending on the age of the bird. Drain the stock, and chop the meat, discarding the bones. Reserve the stock and the chicken meat. Place in the clean soup pan the tomatoes, skinned, seeded and chopped; the corn, the sliced fresh okra, the diced onion, the rice, ½ teaspoon salt, and 1¾ litres (3 pints) water, and simmer covered until the vegetables are tender. If using tinned okra, add at the end of the cooking time. Combine this mixture with the chicken stock and the meat. Correct the seasoning, and serve hot.

Cock-A-Leekie Soup

1 plump chicken   *60 g (2 oz) butter*
3 large leeks   *salt and pepper*

Simmer the cleaned chicken in a good amount of water in a large soup pan. When the chicken is tender, remove it and let the broth cool. Reserve $\frac{1}{4}$ of the chicken, and use the rest for any boiled chicken entrée. Shred the flesh of the $\frac{1}{4}$ chicken. Soften the cleaned white part of the leeks in the butter. When quite soft, add the strained chicken broth. Add the shredded chicken, and heat the mixture until very hot, seasoning to taste.

Cream of Chicken Soup

1 small chicken   *30 g (1 oz) butter*
1 litre (1$\frac{3}{4}$ pints) white stock   *1 tablespoon flour*
2 leeks   *1 litre (1$\frac{3}{4}$ pints) milk*
1 stalk of celery   *140 ml ($\frac{1}{4}$ pint) cream*

Put the chicken into a large soup pan with the white stock. Add white part of the leeks, cleaned and trimmed, and a celery stalk. Bring to the boil, skimming well, and simmer gently for about 1 hour. Sieve, reserving the stock. Cut the chicken meat from the bone into bite-sized pieces, and reserve, discarding the bones and the vegetables. Melt the butter in a clean pan. Stir in the flour, and add the milk gradually, stirring over a medium flame. When the mixture is thick and smooth, stir in the reserved stock and the chicken pieces. Heat to the boiling point, and stir in the cream. Re-heat, but do not boil.

Creamed Corn in Chicken Soup

110 g (4 oz) cooked chicken
2 egg whites
420 ml (¾ pint) white stock
280 ml (½ pint) water
450 g (1 lb) tin creamed corn
1 tablespoon cornflour

2 tablespoons minced cooked ham
2 tablespoons soy sauce
½ teaspoon monosodium
 glutamate (optional)
salt

Combine minced chicken meat, egg whites and half the water in a bowl. Pass through a mouli or blend in an electric liquidizer. Bring stock to the boil in a soup pan, add corn, stir and cook for 3 minutes. Stir in soy sauce. Add chicken mixture slowly, stirring constantly. Thicken with cornflour slaked in the rest of the water. Serve very hot in bowls with a sprinkling of minced ham to top each serving.

La Garbure

½ cabbage
2 onions
2 turnips
3 large potatoes
2 tablespoons goose or duck
 dripping

1 leg or wing roast goose, duck,
 or preserved goose (confit
 d'oie)
450 g (1 lb) salt pork
French bread
cheese, grated

Peel and coarsely chop the onions, turnips and potatoes. Blanch, drain and slice the cabbage. Put the dripping into a large casserole, and brown the onions in it. Add the turnips, the cabbage, and the potatoes. Cover with water, and add the salt pork, which has been previously blanched. Simmer all together until the pork is tender. Remove the pork, and slice it thinly. Pour the contents of the casserole into a large bowl while you wash out the casserole. Now, fill the casserole with alternate layers of sliced French bread and sliced salt pork. Pour over the reserved soup, add the duck or goose, and sprinkle grated cheese on top. Put under the grill to lightly brown the cheese.

Note : previously soaked and cooked haricot beans may be added to the garbure, as can fresh peas, runner or broad beans, tomatoes and leeks. It then becomes more of a stew, and a good example of the sort of thing all soups once were.

Hare Soup

1 hare	*2¼ litres (4 pints)*
1 carrot	* brown stock*
1 onion	*1 tablespoon marjoram*
1 leek	*1 tablespoon basil*
1 slice ham	*1 tablespoon rosemary*
bouquet garni	*pinch cayenne*
85 g (3 oz) butter	*4 tablespoons port wine*
3 tablespoons arrowroot	

Cut the forequarter and one leg of skinned hare into pieces, reserving the rest for some other use. Cook the pieces of hare in 30 g (1 oz) butter with 5 tablespoons of a mirepoix of carrots, onion, white part of leek, chopped ham, and bouquet garni. When all is browned, sprinkle on the arrowroot. Stir, brown lightly, and add the stock. Season and simmer gently for 2½ hours. Remove the *leg* pieces of hare with a perforated spoon, and bone them. Cut the meat into small dice, and keep warm. Moisten with a few tablespoons of stock. Cut the hare's liver into slices, and poach. Now, remove the rest of the hare, and bone it. Add the poached liver to the boned meat, and pound together in a mortar. Then purée the mixture in a blender. Strain the stock, and skim. Flavour it with marjoram, basil and rosemary. Add the remaining butter, and a pinch of cayenne. Put the hare liver purée into a soup tureen, and pour the stock over it. Add the diced hare leg pieces, and lace with port.

Mongole Soup

450 g (1 lb) split peas
1 chicken carcass
1 ham bone
5 medium onions
4 large ribs celery with leaves
3 carrots
1 clove garlic
1 bay leaf

1 teaspoon sugar
a dash cayenne
¼ teaspoon thyme
30 g (1 oz) butter
30 g (1 oz) flour
840 ml (1½ pints) strained
   tomato pulp

Soak the peas overnight, then drain, reserving the liquid. Add enough water to the liquid to make 2½ litres (5 pints). Simmer the peas in this liquid with the chicken carcass and ham bone for about 3½ hours, covered. Add the tomato pulp, the chopped onions, the chopped celery, the chopped carrots, the mashed garlic clove, the bay leaf, sugar, cayenne, and thyme. Simmer for another ½ hour. Remove the bay leaf, and sieve. Cool, and degrease. Melt the butter in a clean pan. Add the flour, and stir until blended. Add the soup gradually, stirring. Bring to the boil, correct the seasoning, and serve very hot with croûtons.

Mulligatawny Soup, English-Style

1¼ kg (3 lb) chicken, jointed
60 g (2 oz) butter
110 g (4 oz) chopped carrots
110 g (4 oz) chopped green
   pepper
2 cooking apples, cored and
   chopped
1 dessertspoon flour

2 teaspoons curry powder
1¾ litres (3 pints) chicken stock
2 cloves
pinch mace
few sprigs parsley
1 dessertspoon sugar
¼ teaspoon pepper
1 dessertspoon salt

Sauté chicken pieces in hot butter until well browned. Stir in carrots, green pepper and apples, and continue cooking, stirring frequently, until mixture is brown. Sprinkle in flour and curry powder. Add stock gradually, then all the remaining ingredients. Bring to the boil, then reduce heat, cover, and simmer gently for about 40 minutes, or until chicken is very tender. Remove chicken from soup, and cool until it can be handled. Strain the soup, working vegetables through the sieve. Return to clean pan, and heat. Strip chicken from bones, discarding bones and skin, and add to soup in shreds. Serve hot, with steamed rice.

Pheasant Broth

1 old pheasant
225 g (8 oz) stewing veal
2 carrots
2 onions
1 stick celery
1 tomato

30 g (1 oz) bacon fat or lard
2 sprigs parsley
1½ litres (2 pints) water
salt and freshly ground black
pepper
2 tablespoons sherry

Cut the veal into cubes. Peel and chop the carrots and onions. Chop the celery and tomato. Heat the fat in a large saucepan. Add the onions and cook until slightly brown. Add the veal and brown on all sides. Add the carrots, celery, tomato, parsley, and the jointed pheasant. Pour over the water. Bring to the boil, reduce heat, and simmer very gently for 3½ hours, skimming. Strain, and leave to get cold. Remove all trace of fat, and strain again through muslin. Heat, season with salt and pepper, and stir in 2 tablespoons sherry.

Potage Saint Hubert

carcass and leftover meat from
*   a partridge, pheasant or*
*   hare*
2 carrots
4 onions
4 sticks celery
1 tomato

60 g (2 oz) diced ham or bacon
1 bay leaf
salt and pepper
bouquet garni
glass of sherry or Madeira
1 egg yolk
140 ml (¼ pint) cream

Cut the meat from the carcass and reserve it. Put the carcass in a large pot along with the chopped carrots, onions, celery, tomato, ham or bacon, bay leaf, bouquet garni. Cover with water, bring to the boil, skim and season lightly, then simmer for one hour, covered. Strain the liquid through a colander into a clean pan. Pick any remaining flesh from the bones, pound it in a mortar, and sieve into the stock. Blend the egg yolk into the cream. Add to this a little hot stock, then pour the mixture into the soup. Add a glass of sherry or Madeira and heat again, but do not boil.

Stracciatelle

2 eggs
1¾ litres (3 pints) good
* chicken stock*

Parmesan cheese
salt and pepper
parsley

Beat the eggs with salt, pepper, and a good sprinkling of Parmesan cheese. Add a handful of chopped parsley. Heat the stock, then pour in the egg mixture, beating vigorously with a fork for 3 or 4 minutes. Serve with a bowl of Parmesan cheese.

CHAPTER FIVE

Meat-Based Soups

BEEF HAS BEEN THE ENGLISHMAN'S food since Eliza-
bethan days, when a dinner of any importance centred
around 'rompye of beff' and 'lownys of welle' (veal) accompanied only by bread and ale. 'Sawltte' there was, and
'wynnegar', which was widely used for disguising the taste
of tainted meat. Contemporary recipe books are full of
suggestions for concealing the strong flavour of stale meat:
some useful, some bizarre. Worth recording is this advice,
offered in 1594 by one 'Hugh Platt, of Lincolnes Inne,
Gentleman' to those confronted with the problem of cooking 'greene' venison: 'Cut out all the bones, and bury it in
a thin olde course cloth a yard deepe in the ground for 12
or 20 hours'. The meat, it was confidently claimed, would
then 'bee sweet enough to be eaten'.

It was not until the 18th century that the simplicity
characteristic of English cooking was complicated by the
influence of French cuisine, with its richness and variety.
Fashionable arbiters of taste seized on the French ways with
delight, arousing a storm of chauvinistic protest epitomized

by Sir Richard Steele's plea in *The Tatler* that 'we return to the diet of our forefathers, the beef and mutton on which we had won the battles of Crécy and Agincourt.'

Early English soups were hearty extracts of boiled beef, with an occasional carrot or cabbage thrown in for flavouring. Potage, or pottage, has long nourished all classes, and it was claimed in a 16th century dietary that 'potage is not so moche vsed in al Crystendom as it is vsed in Englande.'

If, as it was claimed, battles were won on a diet of meat, so invalids were cured on its essence. All sorts of scientific reasons were given for the restorative powers of meat and its extracts, but one suspects that the high protein content was the secret.

Perhaps the most comforting of all meat-based soups is one rarely mentioned today because of the high price of meat: Beef Tea. This soothing broth was allowed us as children whenever we had a temperature exceeding 100°; my mother made it according to her mother's recipe, and it never failed to make us better.

BEEF

Beef Tea

450 g (1 lb) lean rump steak　　　*pinch salt*
280 ml (½ pint) cold water

Cut the steak into small dice, and place in a 1⅛ litre (2 pint) Kilner jar. Add cold water, and a pinch of salt. Cover the jar tightly. Place the jar in a pan of cold water; use as much water as possible without upsetting the jar. Bring the water slowly to the boil, and boil gently for 1 hour. Remove the jar, and place it on a rack to cool. Strain the juice, and store in the refrigerator in a covered container until ready to heat and serve.

Beef Broth with Dumplings

225 g (8 oz) shin of beef	30 g (1 oz) dripping
1⅛ litres (2 pints) stock	110 g (4 oz) self-raising flour
pinch mixed herbs	60 g (2 oz) shredded suet
1 onion	salt
1 carrot	white pepper
1 turnip	1½ tablespoons parsley
1 stick celery	

Finely chop meat, removing any sinews. Combine meat and stock in saucepan, bring to the boil, skim off any scum, and season with salt and pepper. Add mixed herbs, cover and simmer for 45 minutes. Peel and finely chop the onion. Peel and dice carrot and turnip; thinly slice celery. Melt dripping in a saucepan; add vegetables and cook over medium heat, stirring to prevent browning, for 3 minutes. Add vegetables to meat and stock, return to boil, cover and simmer for 40 minutes.

For the dumplings: combine flour and suet, season with salt and pepper, add ½ tablespoon chopped parsley and mix well. Add enough cold water to form a stiff dough, and, using floured hands, form the mixture into small balls. Add dumplings to soup and continue to simmer for further 20 minutes, or until the dumplings rise to the surface. Sprinkle soup with chopped parsley before serving.

Beef Soup with Cabbage and Rice

1¾ litres (3 pints) water	salt and pepper
450 g (1 lb) stewing beef	60 g (2 oz) rice
1 large cabbage	

Pour boiling water over beef, and simmer for about 3 hours, skimming when necessary. Add more boiling water during cooking time, if needed. Strain, reserving the cooking liquor. Cut meat into small dice, and return with cooking liquor to the washed pan. Season well, and add the blanched and finely shredded cabbage. Add rice. Boil for about 15 minutes, covered, and serve.

Hungarian Soup

450 g (1 lb) lean beef
1 large onion
60 g (2 oz) butter
30 g (1 oz) flour
2¼ litres (4 pints) brown stock

225 g (8 oz) diced potatoes
cumin
paprika
garlic
croûtons

Cut the beef into large dice, and brown in the butter with the diced onion. Season with salt, a pinch of paprika, a pinch of cumin, and a crushed clove of garlic. Sprinkle on the flour, and cook for a few minutes, then add the stock. Bring to the boil, and simmer gently for 1 hour. Add the diced potatoes, and simmer until they are just tender. Serve very hot with croûtons.

Minced Meat Soup

1¾ litres (3 pints) water
225 g (8 oz) minced beef
handful of rice
110 g (4 oz) root vegetables

salt
parsley
1 stock cube

Place cleaned and diced vegetables and minced meat in pot with meat cube. Cover with cold water, bring to the boil, and skim. Add rice, bring back to the boil, and simmer for about 25 minutes. Season to taste, and add chopped parsley.

Viennese Beef Soup

1 kg (2¼ lb) lean minced beef
225 g (8 oz) cauliflower
30 g (1 oz) butter
225 g (8 oz) shredded cabbage
1⅛ litres (2 pints) beef stock

1 onion
110 g (4 oz) mushrooms
salt and pepper
croûtons

Melt the butter in a soup pan. Add the chopped cauliflower, the shredded cabbage, the peeled and finely chopped onion, the chopped mushrooms, and the beef. Mix together, cover

the pan, and simmer for about 10 minutes, shaking the pan.
Heat stock to boiling point, and pour over the mixture.
Simmer for a few minutes, skimming. Add salt and pepper
to taste. Serve garnished with croûtons.

Marrow-bone Broth

1 kg (2¼ lb) marrow bones	*2 sticks celery*
1 carrot	*the heart of a white cabbage*
1 onion	*bouquet garni*
1 leek	*salt and pepper.*

Ask the butcher to chop the bones so that they will fit into
a large soup pan. Put the bones into the pan with the
vegetables, which have all been carefully cleaned and
chopped. Pour on cold water to cover, and bring slowly to
the boil. Skim, add salt and pepper, and simmer gently with
the top on the pan for 4 hours. Strain off the liquid without
pressing the vegetables so that you have a clear broth.
Reserve the bones, and use the marrow to make marrow
dumplings (p. 164) to accompany the soup.

LAMB

Cherbah

An Arabian soup, much liked in the bazaars of Algeria and
Tunis.

450 g (1 lb) tomatoes	*sprig of mint*
450 g (1 lb) onions	*2 red peppers*
110 g (4 oz) dried apricots	*handful of vermicelli*
110 g (4 oz) lamb, chopped	

Skin, seed, and coarsely chop tomatoes. Peel and chop
onions. Fry tomatoes and onions lightly in butter with a
large sprig of mint, coarsely chopped. Add the red peppers,

deseeded and cut into slivers. Season well. When slightly browned, add 1⅛ litres (2 pints) hot water, the lamb, and the chopped apricots. Cook all together slowly for 45 minutes, partially covered. Ten minutes before serving, add the vermicelli.

Lamb Soup

450 g (1 lb) lamb	*10 ground peppercorns*
225 g (8 oz) spinach	*few sprigs parsley*
1 bunch spring onions	*2 egg yolks*
85 g (3 oz) butter	*½ teaspoon paprika*
110 g (4 oz) rice	*140 ml (¼ pint) milk*

Cut lamb into dice, and fry lightly in butter. Add chopped spinach and sliced spring onions. Fry for a few minutes more, then add paprika, and water to cover. When meat is nearly cooked, add rice and peppercorns, and simmer until rice is tender. Beat the egg yolks into the milk, and add to the soup, stirring. Heat, but do not boil. Sprinkle each serving with chopped parsley.

Minted Lamb Soup with Almonds

1 kg (2¼ lb) lamb from breast	*2 teaspoons chopped fresh mint*
and neck	*30 g (1 oz) almonds*
2 celery stalks	*bouquet garni*
225 g (8 oz) tomatoes	*salt and pepper*
3 medium onions	

Chop the lamb into small cubes, removing fat. Put into a soup pan with 1¾ litres (3 pints) cold water. Bring to the boil, drain, and pour on fresh cold water. Peel, slice, and cook the onions until golden in a little butter. Add the onions to the soup pan with the peeled, seeded and chopped tomatoes, the sliced celery stalks, the mint, a bouquet garni, and a little salt and pepper. Bring slowly to the boil, skim, then cover and simmer very gently for 3 hours. Remove the meat and cut into small pieces, discarding the bones. Place in the clean pan and strain the broth over the meat. Heat, and stir in the almonds, which have been previously skinned, roasted, and finely chopped.

OFFAL

Brain Soup

1¾ litres (3 pints) water	1 egg yolk
1 calf's brain	85 g (3 oz) root vegetables
85 g (3 oz) butter	parsley
60 g (2 oz) flour	salt
½ onion	

Boil cleaned and diced root vegetables in water until tender. Thicken with light roux of 60 g (2 oz) butter and the flour, and cook for about 30 minutes. Lightly fry blanched and skinned brain in remaining butter with chopped onion. Cut it into bite-sized pieces, and add to the sieved soup with the beaten yolk. Season with salt and chopped parsley. Serve very hot, but do not boil.

Hungarian Liver Soup

1 large onion	1 bay leaf
2 carrots	140 ml (¼ pint) white wine
85 g (3 oz) lean salt pork	1¾ litres (3 pints) brown stock
1 shallot	salt and pepper
450 g (1 lb) calves' liver	nutmeg
30 g (1 oz) butter	30 g (1 oz) flour
sprig of thyme	croûtons

Melt the butter in a saucepan, and add the chopped onion, chopped carrots, diced salt pork, chopped shallot, thyme and a bay leaf. Sweat the vegetables gently for several minutes, then add the diced liver. Season with salt, pepper and nut-

meg, and brown over a fierce flame. Sprinkle with the flour.
Stir until blended, and add the wine and stock. Cook gently
for about ½ hour. Drain the liver and vegetables and pound
them in a mortar. Sieve or blend. Return to the clean pan,
add the cooking liquor, bring to the boil, and serve with
tiny croûtons fried in butter.

Kidney and Vegetable Soup

1⅛ litres (2 pints) chicken stock
450 g (1 lb) lambs' kidneys '
1 stick celery
2 carrots
1 onion

2 potatoes
30 g (1 oz) butter
salt and pepper
soured cream

Remove the fat and membrane from the kidneys, cut them
into quarters, and cover with cold water. Bring to the boil,
drain and refresh the kidneys under cold water, and cover
them with fresh cold water. Bring to the boil, skim, and
simmer for about 45 minutes. Drain, and cut into small thin
slices. Chop the celery and carrots. Peel and chop the
onion. Peel and dice the potatoes. Melt the butter in a thick
saucepan, add the chopped vegetables, and cook over
medium heat without browning for about 5 minutes, until
the butter has been absorbed. Pour over the stock, bring to
the boil, and simmer for 15 minutes. Add the kidneys to the
soup, and reheat. Season with salt and pepper. Serve very
hot with a spoonful of soured cream for each serving.

Soup à la Cardinal

225 g (8 oz) calf's liver
30 g (1 oz) butter
4 slices white bread
30 g (1 oz) Parmesan cheese
1¼ litres (2 pints) beef bouillon
½ tablespoon parsley

pinch cinnamon
pinch nutmeg
1 teaspoon salt
2 tablespoons powdered hazel
* nuts*

Sauté the liver in the butter, then chop it finely. Toast the bread, place it in a soup tureen, and sprinkle the grated Parmesan cheese on top along with the chopped liver. Combine all the rest of the ingredients, bring to the boil, and pour into the soup tureen. Serve immediately.

Viennese Creamed Liver Soup

450 g (1 lb) calf's liver   *1⅛ litres (2 pints) meat stock*
6 tablespoons soured cream   *2 tablespoons flour*
1 large onion   *salt and pepper*
1 tablespoon dripping   *2 bay leaves*

Heat the dripping in a soup pan. Chop the liver coarsely into pieces about 5 cm (2 in) square. Peel and chop the onion very small. Fry liver and onion in the fat, stirring. Stir in the flour. Add stock, bring to the boil, season and add the bay leaves. Cover the pan and simmer for 30 minutes. Remove the liver, mince the pieces, and return to the soup, stirring. Bring the soup to boiling point, and serve with a tablespoon of soured cream on top of each serving.

PORK

Dutch Farmer's Soup

225 g (8 oz) sauerkraut   *2 rashers bacon*
1¾ litres (3 pints) vegetable   *2 small cooked sausages*
  stock   *140 ml (1 gill) cream*
3 potatoes   *1 tablespoon flour*
2 bay leaves   *60 g (2 oz) dried mushrooms*

Cut the peeled potatoes, bacon and mushrooms into small pieces. Place with bay leaves into the stock, and cook gently for 20 minutes. Remove bay leaves, then sieve or blend. Cut sausages into slices, heat them and the sauerkraut in the soup. Add cream blended with flour to thicken the soup. Reheat and serve very hot.

Lithuanian Soup

450 g (1 lb) potatoes
2¼ litres (4 pints) white stock
½ celery heart
2 tablespoons sorrel leaves
85 g (3 oz) butter

280 ml (½ pint) soured cream
1 rasher streaky bacon
8 chipolata sausages
4 egg yolks

Simmer the diced potatoes in the stock until tender. Blend this mixture, and add to it the celery heart, which has been sliced and softened in 60 g (2 oz) butter. Simmer for 30 minutes. At the last minute, add the sorrel leaves, which have been softened in butter, the soured cream, and 1 oz (30 g) butter. Garnish with diced and lightly fried bacon, poached sausages, and the fried egg yolks.

Philadelphia Pepper Pot

4 rashers lean bacon
1 small onion
3 firm stalks celery
2 green peppers
340 g (12 oz) honeycomb tripe
2 litres (3½ pints) white stock
1 bay leaf

½ teaspoon freshly ground pepper
4 medium potatoes
salt
paprika
30g (1 oz) butter
30 g (1 oz) flour
70 ml (½ gill) cream

Dice the bacon and sauté lightly in a smear of butter in a large soup kettle. Add the minced onion, minced celery, and the seeded and minced green peppers. Sauté with the bacon for 5 minutes. Wash the tripe well, cut it into shreds, and add to the pan with the white stock, bay leaf and pepper. Bring to the boil, and simmer, covered, for ½ hour. Add the peeled and diced potatoes, and simmer for another ½ hour, or until tripe and potatoes are tender. In a small pan, melt the butter, stir in the flour, and blend well. Add a little of the hot soup, bring to the boil, and add to the soup in the kettle. Season with salt and paprika, and add the warmed cream just before serving.

Pig's Head Soup

1¾ litres (3 pints) water   *30 g (1 oz) groats*
half a pig's head   *salt*
60 g (2 oz) root vegetables   *drop of meat extract*
handful dried mushrooms

Wash the pig's head well, and boil in salted water together
with root vegetables and mushrooms until soft. Take out
the meat, remove all bones, and cut it into small pieces.
Add the pieces of meat to the soup with groats and meat
extract, and boil for a few minutes. Serve with German rye
bread and unsalted butter.

Smoked Meat Soup

1¾ litres (3 pints) stock from   *110 g (4 oz) root vegetables*
  cooked ham or smoked meat   *parsley*
30 g (1 oz) flour   *2 tablespoons semolina*
30 g (1 oz) lard   *1 frankfurter sausage*

Make light brown roux from fat removed from stock, lard
and flour. Pour the stock over the roux and mix until
blended. Add diced vegetables, and boil lightly for 10
minutes. Add semolina, small pieces of frankfurter or
chopped smoked meat, and finely chopped parsley, and
simmer together until semolina is cooked.

VEAL

Cream of Veal Soup with Peas

1¾ litres (3 pints) water   *60 g (2 oz) butter*
450 g (1 lb) neck of veal   *bread rolls*
60 g (2 oz) flour   *fat for frying*
225 g (8 oz) fresh or frozen   *salt*
  peas

Simmer veal in salted water until tender, skimming. Remove bones, sinews and gristle, and cut into small pieces; add, with the cooking liquor, to a light roux made from the flour and butter. Whisk well and simmer for a few minutes. Add peas, simmer for several minutes, or until peas are just cooked. Serve with fried croûtons made from the rolls.

CHAPTER SIX

Main Course Soups

SOUPS ORIGINALLY WERE MAIN COURSES. The name supper (originally *souper*), dates from the Middle Ages, when the last meal of the day was served as early as 5 p.m., and it was customary to serve soup. Early soups were substantial dishes consisting of liquid food both sweet and savoury, such as frumenty, porridge, and so-called spoon meat, which was eaten with pieces of bread called sops or sippets.

Many of these soups were stodgy affairs, combining ingredients of a doubtful affinity, thickened with bread, oats or barley, peas or beans. Chaucer talks of mortrewès, in which the ingredients are hens and pork 'hewn small, and grounde alle to doust', then mixed with breadcrumbs, egg yolks and pepper. This unlikely mess was then boiled with ginger, sugar, salt and saffron before it was eaten, one presumes, by pilgrims with strong stomachs.

Pease-pudding and baked beans with bacon have been eaten for centuries by country people in England. Farm labourers in Scotland and the north of England traditionally fared well on a diet consisting mainly of porridge, milk and vegetable broth. The diet of rich and poor alike improved during Tudor times, when the introduction of Flemish market gardening skills revolutionized vegetable growing in England. Potatoes found their way into the country in the 16th century, and while they were not initially much prized in the south, they provided a useful alternative to wheat in lean years.

Today's main course soups are refinements of early porridges and stews: cassoulet from baked beans and bacon; pot-au-feu from the old-fashioned stock pot. Some, like La Garbure, are more suitable for a simple family lunch; others are worthy of a place above the salt.

FISH

Botvinya

1 kg (2¼ lb) firm white fish	*1 lemon*
450 g (1 lb) spinach	*horseradish*
1 cucumber	*spring onions*
2 lettuce hearts	*dill*
110 g (4 oz) crayfish tails	*140 ml (¼ pint) sour cream*

Poach crayfish tails in acidulated water for about 5 minutes. Cool and shell. Cook the fish gently in salted water with the juice of the lemon until tender. Drain, and leave to get cold. Cook the washed spinach, drain it, and mouli or blend. Chill the purée. Cut the cucumber into strips and put them in a colander sprinkled with salt to drain for ½ hour. Season the spinach purée with salt, pepper, a hint of sugar and lemon zest. Put a bit into each soup bowl. Remove bones from the fish, cut it into neat portions, and distribute on the spinach purée. Surround the fish with crayfish tails, lettuce, spring onions, cucumber, a bit of grated horseradish, and chopped dill. Hand a bowl of soured cream.

Bourride

1¼ kg (3 lb) firm white fish (monkfish, turbot or John Dory)	bouquet of herbs (including fennel, thyme, parsley, bay leaf)
2 large chopped onions	450 g (1 lb) potatoes, sliced
1 chopped leek	salt, pepper
4 cloves garlic	140 ml (¼ pint) ailloli (see below)
strips of orange peel	
2 tomatoes	

For garnish: 12 slices French bread, toasted lightly, fried in olive oil, and rubbed with garlic.

Clean and bone the fish and cut into big slices. Put onions, leek, garlic, tomatoes and potatoes into a large pot. Place the fish on top with the herbs, orange peel, and seasoning. Add water to cover, or stock made from the heads and bones of the fish. Bring to the boil and simmer gently for 10 minutes. Carefully remove fish and potatoes to a warm plate. Boil the liquid hard to less than 560 ml (1 pint). Correct the seasoning, and strain slowly on to the *ailloli*, mixing the two together carefully with a wire whisk. Wash out the cooking pot, and put in the *ailloli* mixture, stirring over very low heat until it thickens slightly. Pour over the fish, sprinkle with parsley, and serve accompanied by the fried bread.

Ailloli: 2–4 garlic cloves	140 ml (¼ pint) olive oil
salt	pepper
1 egg yolk	lemon juice

Crush the garlic with a little salt in a mortar. Add the egg yolks, mixing well, followed by the olive oil, drop by drop at first, as in making mayonnaise, then add pepper and lemon juice to taste.

Cotriade

1¼ kg (3 lb) fish (cod, haddock,
    sea bass), cut into chunks
4 large potatoes
2 large onions

1¼ litres (2½ pints) fish stock
¼ teaspoon marjoram
bouquet garni
salt and pepper

Make stock with the heads, bones, and trimmings of the
fish. Strain it, and place in a soup kettle. Add the sliced
potatoes, sliced onion, marjoram, bouquet garni, salt and
pepper, and simmer for 20 minutes. Add the fish and sufficient water to cover it, and cook gently until potatoes are
just tender (about 15 minutes). Remove the fish and potatoes, and serve hot in a separate dish. Sieve the soup, and
serve in earthenware bowls with fried croûtons. Serve
garlicky French dressing for the fish.

Cotriade de Maquereaux

4 mackerel
85 g (3 oz) butter
4 potatoes
4 onions

4 tomatoes
chopped parsley, thyme and
    bay leaf
fish stock

Melt the butter in a large casserole, and add the peeled and
chopped potatoes and onions, and the peeled, seeded and
chopped tomatoes. Sprinkle generously with fresh herbs.
Skin and fillet the mackerel, and lay the fillets on top of the
vegetable mixture. Cover with fish stock made from the
head, bones and skin of the mackerel. Cover the casserole,
and cook in a moderate oven for about ½ hour, or until the
fish and vegetables are tender, and the stock reduced to a
sauce.

Lobster Stew

1 lobster	*salt*
45 g (1½ oz) butter	*paprika*
1⅛ litres (2 pints) milk, scalded	*140 ml (¼ pint) clam broth*
with an onion slice	*parsley, basil, or tarragon*

Remove the meat from the body and claws of a boiled lobster. Discard the sac behind the head and the intestinal vein. Cut the meat into large dice, and sauté it for 3 or 4 minutes in the butter. Add the scalded milk, and the clam broth and a pinch of paprika. Taste for seasoning, and add salt, if necessary, 2 tablespoons chopped parsley or 1 teaspoon dried basil or tarragon. Serve very hot.

Oyster Stew

60 g (2 oz) butter	*140 ml (¼ pint) cream*
560 ml (1 pint) oysters with	*salt and pepper or paprika*
liquor	*chopped parsley*
280 ml (½ pint) milk	

In the top of a bain-marie, combine the butter, oysters, milk, cream, ½ teaspoon salt and ⅛ teaspoon paprika or pepper. Place the pan over boiling water, and when the butter has melted, the milk is hot, and the oysters are floating, add 2 tablespoons chopped parsley, and serve with water biscuits or oyster crackers.

Provence Fish Soup

1 kg (2¼ lb) firm white fish	*2 sprigs parsley*
(lemon sole or halibut)	*1 sprig fennel*
1 leek	*1 bay leaf*
1 large onion	*1 slice lemon peel*
4 tomatoes	*French bread*
6 potatoes	*salt and freshly ground*
olive oil	*black pepper*
2 cloves garlic	

Cut fish into chunks, extracting bones. Place in a large soup pot with the chopped white part of the leek, the chopped onion, the skinned, seeded and chopped tomatoes, the potatoes peeled and cut into thick slices. Season with salt and pepper, add crushed garlic, parsley, fennel, bay leaf, and lemon peel. Cover with boiling water and cook at a good simmer for about 20 minutes. Place 1 slice French bread for each person into a soup tureen (or individual earthenware bowls), sprinkle with olive oil and pepper. Strain the soup over the bread, reserving the solid bits of fish and vegetables, which you will serve separately with rouille.

Rouille: *½ slice white bread*
2 cloves garlic   *2 tablespoons olive oil*
2 hot red peppers   *140 ml (¼ pint) fish stock*

Pound the cloves of garlic in a mortar with the hot peppers and the crustless white bread, which you have first dipped in water and squeezed dry. Blend until smooth with the oil, then pound this paste with the fish stock until about the consistency of heavy cream.

MEAT

Bread Soup with Eggs

6 slices stale bread   *1 tablespoon chopped parsley*
1 litre (1¾ pints) veal stock   *225 g (8 oz) smoked meat or*
3 eggs   *sausages*
a little butter

Use end crusts of bread, or dry the pieces in the oven; they should be really dry. Warm the stock. Break each piece of bread into six pieces. Put in a large saucepan, and pour the stock over. Leave for about 15 minutes, then place over heat and bring to the boil. Season, and reduce heat until soup is barely simmering. Simmer for 30 minutes. Mash with a wooden spoon any large bits of bread. Break the yolk of 1 egg into a bowl and beat. Blend in a little soup stock.

Remove the soup from the fire, and carefully stir in the egg mixture. Keep hot, but do not boil. Hard boil 2 eggs. Fry the sausages. Fry the parsley in a little butter for a few minutes. Slice the hard-boiled eggs, and add them with the sliced sausages (or smoked meat) to the soup. Leave for 2 minutes. Sprinkle with parsley and serve.

Cassoulet
For 8 people

*1 kg (2¼ lb) haricot beans,
  soaked overnight*
1 garlic boiling sausage
1 kg (2¼ lb) pork spare rib
675 g (1½ lb) breast of lamb
225 g (8 oz) salt pork

*225 g (8 oz) preserved goose
  (confit d'oie)*
1 onion
2 cloves garlic
bouquet garni
salt and pepper
breadcrumbs

Remove the rind of the pork spare rib and salt pork, and cut into small squares. Put the rind in a large saucepan with the salt pork and soaked beans. Add the onion, the bouquet garni and the crushed garlic cloves, cover with water, and simmer for about 1½ hours, or until the beans are almost tender. In the meantime, bone the lamb breast, and roast it along with the pork spare rib for about 30 minutes in a moderate oven. Add the boiling sausage to the beans for the last half hour of cooking. Drain the beans, reserving their liquid. Discard the bouquet and onion. Put a layer of the beans and rind into a deep earthenware dish. Cover this layer with the sausage, cut into 5 cm (2 in) lengths, the chopped lamb and pork spare rib. Add the preserved goose, and cover with the rest of the beans. Moisten with the bean liquor, and spread a layer of breadcrumbs on top. Place the dish in a low oven for another hour or an hour and a half. The breadcrumbs will form a golden crust, and the beans should remain moist. If the dish seems to be drying up too much, add more bean liquor during the cooking time.

Gulyas Soup

1 kg (2¼ lb) shin of beef	*bouquet garni*
450 g (1 lb) onions	*30 g (1 oz) paprika*
60 g (2 oz) lard or pork fat	*a glass of red wine*
450 g (1 lb) potatoes	*1⅛ litres (2 pints) water or*
450 g (1 lb) tomatoes	*stock*
2 green peppers	*12 coriander seeds*
1 tablespoon flour	*6 allspice*
1 clove garlic	

Slice the onions, and brown them in a heavy saucepan in the melted fat. Trim any fat or gristle from the meat, and cut into 5 cm (2 in) cubes. Crush the coriander seeds and the allspice in a mortar. Add crushed garlic, salt, and paprika pepper. Roll the pieces of meat in this powder, then in flour, and fry for a few minutes with the onions. Cut up the tomatoes, slice the green peppers, and put into the pan. Pour on the red wine, reduce slightly, then add the hot water or stock with the bouquet garni. Bring to the boil, lower the heat, and let it simmer, covered, for 2 hours, or until the meat is very tender. Half an hour before serving, cut the peeled potatoes into thin slices, and cook them in the soup.

La Habada

This is a hefty Spanish counterpart of pot-au-feu, substituting salt meats for fresh beef and chicken, and haricot beans (haba is bean in Spanish) for root vegetables. It is really not worth making for less than eight people.

1 kg (2¼ lb) salt beef	*450 g (1 lb) black pudding*
1 kg (2¼ lb) piece ham	*6 smoked beef sausages*
or bacon	*1 kg (2¼ lb) haricot beans*

Soak the meats and the haricot beans overnight. Put the drained meats into a large stock pot, cover with fresh cold

water and bring to the boil. Lower the heat, and simmer for
2½ hours. While the meat is cooking, cook the beans in fresh
unsalted water for about 1 hour, or until tender but not
falling apart. When the meats have cooked for 1½ hours, add
the black pudding and the sausages. Taste for seasoning,
and add black pepper. Salt will probably be unnecessary.
Fifteen minutes before the dish is to be served, add the
haricot beans to the pot, and taste again for seasoning.
Strain off the soup, and serve it as a first course, followed
by the beef, ham, sausages, black pudding and beans,
neatly arranged on a large platter.

La Petite Marmite

450 g (1 lb) top rump beef	*necks, wing tips, gizzards,*
225 g (8 oz) rib of beef	*hearts of two chickens*
110 g (4 oz) marrow-bones	*2 leeks*
3 medium carrots	*2 onions*
1 turnip	*½ head celery*
	¼ head cabbage

Put the meat and the marrow bone (wrapped in muslin)
into an appropriately-sized stock pot. Add 2¼ litres (4 pints)
cold water, and bring slowly to the boil. Skim. Pour on a
little cold water to bring up more scum, and skim again.
Add the trimmed and blanched vegetables (white part of
leeks only), and skim again. Simmer very gently for about
4 hours. One hour before serving, add the chicken giblets,
which may be browned in the oven first. When ready to
serve, take out the wrapped marrow bone, unwrap it, and
put back into the pot. Remove most of the fat from the
surface. Serve with slices of toast for the marrow. You may
cook the cabbage in a separate pan, and for a short time
only. It is then drained, and served with the soup. Strain
the stock, leaving only the marrow bone, and reserve the
other meats for another course, accompanied by a garlic
mayonnaise or any of the sauces listed under Pot-au-Feu
(p. 73).

Lamb Terrapin Soup

340 g (12 oz) cold cooked lamb
2 hard-boiled eggs
2 tablespoons olive oil
1 tablespoon lemon juice
30 g (1 oz) butter

3 tablespoons flour
1 teaspoon dry mustard
560 ml (1 pint) stock
1 teaspoon Worcestershire sauce
salt

Dice the lamb. Chop the eggs. Combine the eggs and lamb in a bowl with the lemon juice and olive oil. Melt the butter in a big pan. Stir in the flour and mustard. Slowly add the stock, stirring all the time. Bring to the boil, add the Worcestershire sauce and season to taste. Stir in the egg and lamb mixture, and heat again.

Meat Balls Soup

450 g (1 lb) ground pork loin
2 tablespoons spring onions
2 eggs
1¾ litres (3 pints) brown stock
1 lettuce

2 tablespoons soy sauce
1 teaspoon sugar
¼ teaspoon ground ginger
1 tablespoon sherry
salt

Mix thoroughly the ground pork, finely chopped spring onions, lightly beaten eggs and seasonings. Make 2½ cm (1 in) balls with this mixture. Add meat balls to boiling stock in soup kettle. Lower the heat, cover, and simmer for 20 minutes, or until meat balls float to the top. Add shredded lettuce 3 minutes before soup is done. Serve hot from a tureen, or in individual bowls.

New England Boiled Dinner

2 kg (4½ lb) *pickled beef*
  brisket
450 g (1 lb) *pickled pork*
2 bay leaves
6 peppercorns
1 boiling chicken
6 large carrots, scraped
6 medium onions, peeled

6 large potatoes, peeled
2 medium turnips, peeled and
  quartered
1 medium head cabbage,
  quartered
2 medium beetroot, quartered
horseradish sauce
pickles

Wipe the beef with a damp cloth, tie into shape, and put into a large cooking pot. Add cold water to cover, and bring to the boil. Drain and rinse. Do this twice. Cover brisket with boiling water, add pork, bay leaves and peppercorns; cover and simmer over low heat for 3 to 4 hours, or until meat is tender. Add the chicken after the first hour. Cool, skim off fat, and add carrots, onions, potatoes and turnips. Cook for 20 minutes, then add cabbage and cook until all vegetables are just tender. Cook the beetroot separately. Serve the beef, pork and chicken on a big platter, surrounded by the vegetables. Accompany with horseradish sauce and pickles. The strained broth may be served separately as a first course.

Horseradish sauce: beat 140 ml (¼ pint) double cream until fairly stiff, then stir in ½ teaspoon salt, a few grains cayenne, 2–4 tablespoons grated horseradish, and 4 teaspoons vinegar.

Oxtail Soup

1 disjointed oxtail	*5 firm celery stalks*
1 large onion	*1 bay leaf*
60 g (2 oz) butter	*4 tablespoons barley*
1¾ litres (3 pints) water	*1 small tin plum tomatoes*
1½ teaspoons salt	*(225 g/8 oz)*
4 peppercorns	*1 teaspoon mixed herbs*
3 tablespoons chopped parsley	*1 tablespoon flour*
2 carrots	*70 ml (½ gill) sherry*

Brown the pieces of oxtail and the sliced onion in 30 g (1 oz)
butter. Bring the water to the boil in a large soup kettle,
and add the oxtail mixture, the salt and the peppercorns.
Simmer, covered, for about 4 hours. Add the parsley, the
diced carrots, the diced celery, the bay leaf, the barley, the
tomatoes, and the herbs, and simmer ½ hour longer. Strain
the stock, reserving the meat. Remove bones from the meat.
Chill the stock, and skim off the fat. In the clean pan, brown
1 tablespoon flour blended with 30 g (1 oz) butter. Add the
stock slowly, and the meat. Make very hot, and lace with
sherry just before serving.

Oxtail and Noodle Soup

1 kg (2¼ lb) oxtails	*¼ teaspoon pepper*
6 spring onions	*⅛ teaspoon crushed rosemary*
2 stalks of celery	*1⅛ litre (2 pints) beef stock*
1 carrot	*70 ml (½ gill) dry red wine*
¼ teaspoon thyme	*1 tablespoon tomato paste*
¼ teaspoon marjoram	*110 g (4 oz) egg noodles*
1 teaspoon salt	

Cut the oxtails into 5 cm (2 in) pieces, and roast in a pre-
heated oven (450°F, Regulo 8) for 30 minutes. Add the
chopped onions, chopped carrot, chopped celery, 1 teaspoon
salt, the thyme, marjoram and pepper, and the crushed
rosemary. Stir all together and continue to roast for another
10 minutes. Transfer the mixture to a soup kettle, add

560 ml (1 pint) water to the roasting pan and deglaze. Add this liquid to the kettle with the beef stock and red wine. Stir in the tomato paste, and bring all to the boil. Reduce the heat and simmer the mixture, covered, for 1½ hours. Remove the cover, and simmer for 1½ hours more, or until the meat is very tender. Strain through a colander into a saucepan. Discard the vegetables, remove the meat from the bones, and chop it. Skim the fat from the broth, add the meat to the pan, and bring the broth to a simmer. Add the noodles, which you have previously boiled for 4 minutes, and simmer the soup for 3 minutes more, or until the noodles are cooked. Season to taste.

Polish Borshch

30 g (1 oz) butter
1 medium onion
2 leeks
¼ cabbage
450 g (1 lb) raw beetroot
1 stalk celery
1 parsnip
2¼ litres (4 pints) white stock

1 small duck
450 g (1 lb) beef brisket
110 g (4 oz) back bacon
5 chipolata sausages
bouquet garni with marjoram and fennel
280 ml (½ pint) soured cream

Cut into julienne the onion, white part of leeks, cabbage, beetroot, celery, and parsnip. Soften these ingredients gently in the butter. Add the stock. Brown the duck in the oven for about 20 to 30 minutes, and add to the soup. Blanch the brisket and the bacon, and add. Add the bouquet garni, bring to the boil, skim, and simmer gently for about an hour, or until all the meats are cooked, removing the duck and the bacon as soon as they are done. Fifteen minutes before the end of cooking time, add the chipolata sausages. Finally, remove all the meats. Cut the duck breast into slices, slice the beef and dice the bacon, and cut the sausages into little rounds. You may serve the soup with all the vegetables in it, or sieve it. Serve the meats in a separate dish, and hand round a sauceboat of soured cream.

Pot-Au-Feu

Pot-au-feu made with a piece of beef, a piece of ham, and an old hen, boiled up with root vegetables makes a satisfying homely dinner. The following sumptuous version is ample for 12, and it is well worth the time and trouble it takes to prepare. It is called,

Potée Normande

2 kg (4½ lb) boneless rump steak, flank, silverside, chuck or brisket

2 kg (4½ lb) collar pork or gammon hock

a fine boiling fowl

1 kg (2¼ lb) Polish boiling sausage
12 carrots
12 onions
12 turnips
12 leeks

For the soup:
3 carrots
3 onions stuck with a clove
2 parsnips
2 celery stalks
2 leeks
bouquet garni

4 garlic cloves
1½ litres (2 pints) beef or chicken stock
raw or browned meat scraps, chicken bones, beef or veal bones

Start the cooking 5 hours before you expect to serve the meal. You will need a large cooking pot to hold all the ingredients. Trim the excess fat off the beef and ham. Tie each piece, and truss the chicken. Tie a string to each of these ingredients so that you can haul them out periodically to test for doneness. Peel the carrots and turnips and quarter them, peel the onions, trim and wash the leeks (white parts only). Tie the vegetables in one or more bundles of washed muslin so that they may be removed separately.

For the soup: scrape the carrots, peel the onions, and stick a whole clove in each. Scrape the parsnips, cut most of the green part away from the leeks, and wash well. Place the beef in the pan with the soup vegetables, herbs, and bones and scraps. Cover with stock by 15 cm (6 in). Bring to simmering point, and skim. Partially cover the pan, and simmer slowly for 1 hour, skimming. Add the pork and chicken, and bring all quickly back to simmering point. Skim. Simmer 1½ hours more, and skim from time to time. Add the prepared vegetables. Bring the mixture quickly back to simmering point. Adjust the seasoning. Simmer 1½ to 2 hours more, adding the sausage half an hour before the end. Test the various ingredients as the Potée cooks. The meats and chicken are done when they are tender when pierced with a sharp-pronged fork. The vegetables should not be overcooked, so test them after an hour's simmering. Remove any piece which is tender to a bowl, and keep moist with ladles of stock. It will be returned to the pan to be reheated before serving. If the Potée is ready before you are, it will stay warm for 45 minutes in the pot, or it may be reheated. While the pan simmers, prepare one or both of the following sauces:

Sauce Alsacienne

2 eggs
1 tablespoon made mustard
½ teaspoon salt
1 tablespoon wine vinegar or lemon juice
280 ml (½ pint) oil

70 ml (½ gill) cream, sour cream, or stock
1 tablespoon shallots or spring onions
3 tablespoons chopped parsley tarragon or dill

Boil the eggs for 3 minutes. Put the yolks in a mixing bowl, and set aside the whites. Beat the yolks until thick, then beat in the mustard, salt and vinegar or lemon juice. Finally, beat in the oil, drop by drop until an emulsion is formed; then you may go faster, as with mayonnaise. When all the oil is incorporated, beat in the cream or stock slowly, then add the rest of the ingredients, mixing all thoroughly. Season to taste.

Sauce Nénette

280 ml (½ pint) cream
¼ teaspoon salt
1 teaspoon dry English mustard

2 tablespoons tomato paste
2 tablespoons basil, chervil or parsley
pepper

Simmer the cream, salt and a pinch of pepper in a small saucepan for 8 to 10 minutes, or until reduced by one-third. Beat the mustard and tomato paste together in a small bowl, then beat in the hot cream. Stir in the herbs.

When the sauces are made, and the Potée is cooked, drain the meats and the vegetables, discarding strings and cloths. Arrange the serving vegetables on a large hot dish and moisten with a ladleful of stock. Decorate with snipped parsley. Carve slices from the meats, and slice the breast and a few leg and wing pieces from the chicken, and arrange on the dish with the vegetables. Reserve and keep warm the remainder for extra helpings. Serve the excellent stock in which the Potée has cooked, sieved, as a soup course. Pass a sauce-boat of the stock with the main dish along with the sauces.

Poule Au Pot Henry IV

1 fine young chicken
110 g (4 oz) minced fresh pork
110 g (4 oz) lean ham or green bacon
110 g (4 oz) dry breadcrumbs
2 cloves garlic
2 tablespoons chopped parsley

½ teaspoon dried tarragon
1 large egg
salt
pepper
milk
liver of the chicken

Dice the ham or bacon, and mix with the minced pork. Dice the chicken liver and add to the mixture with bread-crumbs, minced garlic, parsley, tarragon and the beaten egg. Moisten with a little milk to make a fairly light force-

meat. Season with pepper and salt, and stuff the chicken.
Sew up openings, and truss.

For the pot:

chicken giblets, except liver   *2 turnips*
1 knuckle of veal   *1 onion stuck with a clove*
2 carrots   *bouquet garni*
2 leeks

Put the giblets and the veal knuckle in a pot large enough
to contain the chicken. Cover with cold water and bring
slowly to the boil. Skim. Add the trimmed and washed
vegetables (white part of leeks only), and bouquet garni,
and simmer, covered, for 1 hour. Put the stuffed chicken in
the pot, cover, and poach for another hour, or until tender.
Do not boil; the bouillon should simply shiver.

For the garnish:

225 g (8 oz) tiny carrots   *450 g (1 lb) new potatoes*
225 g (8 oz) tiny turnips   *450 g (1 lb) green beans*
450 g (1 lb) pickling onions

Trim the carrots and turnips, peel the onions and potatoes,
and top and tail the beans. Cook all of these vegetables
separately in a little salted water until just tender. Drain
them, and add butter, salt and pepper. Place in clusters
surrounding the chicken on a large platter. You may carve
the chicken and arrange it in the centre of the platter before
arranging the garnishes of vegetables. Serve the bouillon
in which the chicken was cooked as a first course, after
straining off the stock vegetables. The chicken will be even
better if coated with a sauce Velouté made with some of the
bouillon.

Queen Victoria Soup

15 g (½ oz) butter	*225 g (8 oz) diced cooked*
1 teaspoon minced onion	*chicken*
110 g (4 oz) mushrooms, thinly	*salt and pepper*
sliced	*sage*
4 sticks celery, diced	*nutmeg*
1 litre (1¾ pints) chicken stock	*2 hard-boiled eggs*
1 tablespoon tapioca	*280 ml (½ pint) cream*
225 (8 oz) diced cooked ham	*chopped parsley*

Melt the butter; stir in the onion and cook until pale gold. Add the mushrooms and celery and cook gently for 10 minutes. Add the stock, tapioca, chicken, ham and seasonings. Simmer for 20 minutes. Add the finely chopped hard boiled eggs and the cream. Heat again, but do not boil. Serve with chopped parsley sprinkled on top.

Scotch Broth

675 g (1½ lb) neck of lamb	*3 leeks or 1 large onion*
1¾ litres (3 pints) cold water	*1 turnip*
45 g (1½ oz) pearl barley,	*salt and pepper*
soaked overnight	*1 tablespoon chopped parsley*
1 carrot	

Chop the lamb into small pieces, removing as much fat as possible. Put it into the water in a large soup pan, and bring slowly to the boil, skimming. Add the barley, season well with salt, cover and simmer for 30 minutes. Cut the vegetables into small dice, and add them to the soup and continue to simmer for 1½ hours, until the meat is tender. Remove all bones, and cut the meat into uniform bits. Return it to the soup with the parsley. Skim fat from the surface, and season with freshly ground black pepper. Heat thoroughly before serving.

Spare Rib Turnip Soup

675 g (1½ lb) turnips	½ teaspoon ground ginger
675 g (1½ lb) spare ribs	¼ teaspoon pepper
1¾ litres (3 pints) water	salt

Peel the turnips, and chop them into 2½ cm (1 in) squares. Chop the spare ribs into 2½ cm (1 in) pieces. Bring the water to the boil in a large soup pan, and add spare ribs and seasonings. Boil for 5 minutes, then reduce heat and simmer for 40 minutes. Skim as necessary. Add turnips and continue to simmer for 30 minutes, or until meat and vegetables are tender. Remove the bones from the meat, and return it to the soup. Reheat, and serve very hot.

PASTA

Caraway Soup

1 heaped teaspoon caraway seeds	30 g (1 oz) butter
1½ tablespoons flour	225 g (8 oz) macaroni
1¾ litres (3 pints) boiling water	salt and pepper

Heat butter in a large saucepan. When melted, blend in flour and brown lightly. Stir in caraway seeds. Add the boiling water slowly to the roux, stirring. Add a seasoning of salt, and simmer for 30 minutes. Cook macaroni in separate pan for 10 minutes in plenty of boiling salted water. Drain, and cut with scissors into small pieces. Strain the soup and return to a clean saucepan. Combine macaroni with soup, bring to the boil, and serve.

Pasta e Fagioli

*225 g (8 oz) dried kidney or
   haricot beans, soaked overnight*
1 beef marrow bone
4 tablespoons tomato paste
1 Spanish onion
1 clove garlic

3 tablespoons olive oil
2 tablespoons parsley
1 tablespoon oregano
*225 g (8 oz) macaroni, broken
   into pieces*
salt, pepper and cayenne
Parmesan cheese

Soak the beans overnight. Drain them, and combine in a
soup kettle with the marrow bone, tomato paste, and 2¼
litres (4 pints) water. Bring to the boil, lower heat, cover
and simmer gently for about 2 hours. Test the beans from
time to time, as cooking time will depend on their age. When
beans are tender but not falling apart, add the finely
chopped onion and garlic, which have been sautéed in oil
until transparent. Add finely-chopped parsley, salt, pepper,
cayenne and oregano, and simmer all together, covered, for
about 20 minutes. Add macaroni, and continue cooking
until tender, about 15 minutes. Serve sprinkled with
Parmesan cheese.

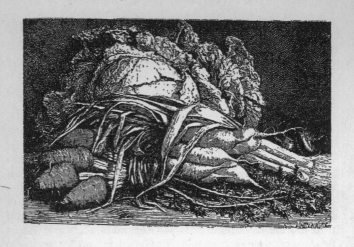

CHAPTER SEVEN

Vegetable Soups

IN THIS GREEN AND PLEASANT land of allotment holders
and keen gardeners, it is hardly credible that vegetable
growing on a wide scale is of relatively recent origin.
Vegetables have been cultivated in diverse parts of the
world from earliest times. Pea seeds were found in the
remains of Bronze Age lake dwellings in Switzerland, and
dried peas were referred to in the Old Testament Book of
Samuel as 'parched pulse'.

Onions have long been held in high repute as a remedy
for human ailments, Pliny having compiled a list of twenty-
eight ills that could be treated by the versatile bulb. Parsnips, which have been grown in the Rhine Valley for
centuries, were imported to Rome for Emperor Titus, and
Emperor Tiberius demanded that cucumbers be placed
on his table every day.

Parsley was used by the ancient Greeks to make wreaths

for victorious athletes. King Darius of Persia ate garden lettuce before 500 B.C., 2000 years before it was commonly used in English salads. Leeks are among the earliest known English vegetables, and apocryphally, they were worn in Celtic hats before they were eaten.

Medieval English manuscripts rarely mention vegetables, with the exception of garlic, leeks, onions and cabbages, although manors and monasteries had herb gardens and orchards. It appears from a passage in Harrison's *Description of England* (1577) that vegetables were popular in the 13th and 14th centuries, but fell out of favour subsequently. 'Such herbes, fruits, and roots also, as grow yeerelie out of the ground, of seed, haue been verie plentifull in this land in the time of the first Edward, and after his daies: but in processe of time they grew also to be neglected, so that from Henrie the fourth till the latter end of Henrie the seuenth, and beginning of Henrie the eight, there was little or no vse of them in England, but they remained either vnknowne, or supposed as food more meet for hogs & sauage beasts to feed vpon, than mankind.'

An earlier manuscript refers to 'rotys (roots) for a gardyne,' and singles out 'parsenepys', 'turnepez', 'karettes', and 'betes', but most kitchen gardens of the day were chiefly stocked with herbs. It was not until the end of the 15th century that Dutch expertise was applied to English market gardening, although the raising of vegetables, particularly of lettuce and salad plants had been a thriving industry in Holland for at least 100 years. Covent Garden was licensed as premises for the sale of fruit and vegetables in 1670, by which time market gardens were springing up on the outskirts of the more important English towns.

Vegetables gradually became more widely available, but there is little evidence that they were used other than in soup until the 18th century. Even the potato, which had become a staple in Ireland, rarely appeared in England, perhaps because of a general prejudice in favour of bread. This prejudice is reflected by an anonymous writer in a contemporary journal, 'As to potatoes it would be idle to consider them as an article of human food which ninety-nine hundredths of the human species will not touch.'

Happily, vegetables are much more esteemed in England today, although they still tend to be served as an accompaniment to meat, fish or poultry, and not, as in France, on their own as a separate course. Vegetables make wonderful soup. It is only a pity that so many generations of Englishmen never tasted a vegetable soup other than Caboches in Potage.

Cream of Almond Soup with French Beans

15 g (½ oz) butter
15 g (½ oz) flour
280 ml (½ pint) white stock
560 ml (1 pint) milk

60 g (2 oz) ground almonds
1 egg yolk
handful cooked French beans
croûtons

Melt butter in saucepan, and stir in flour. Mix well and add white stock and half the milk, stirring. Add almonds. Let all come to the boil, then simmer for 15 minutes. Add cooked French beans, and finally, the rest of the milk, in which the yolk of an egg has been mixed. Stir all the time until hot, but do not boil. Serve with croûtons.

Artichoke Cream Soup

¾ litre (1¼ pints) Béchamel
*   sauce*
4 large cooked globe artichokes
280 ml (½ pint) milk or stock

140 ml (¼ pint) whipped
*   cream*
salt and pepper
paprika
nut of butter

Remove leaves and hay from artichokes; mash the hearts. Add to Béchamel sauce, beating until smooth. Add the milk or stock, heat, adjust seasoning and add whipped cream and butter. Serve sprinkled with a little paprika.

White Artichoke Soup

450 g (1 lb) frozen or tinned   *420 ml (¾ pint) chicken broth*
  artichoke hearts   *420 ml (¾ pint) single cream*

Cut the artichokes into small pieces and simmer with the chicken broth in a covered saucepan for ½ hour. Strain through a fine sieve, or liquidize. Return to the clean pan, and add the cream. Reheat, but do not boil.

Potage Crème d'Artichauts

8 large artichoke hearts   *280 ml (½ pint) white stock*
60 g (2 oz) butter   *280 ml (½ pint) cream*
15 g (½ oz) flour   *1 tablespoon chervil*
1 litre (1¾ pints) milk

Blanch and slice the artichoke hearts. Cook gently in half the butter for 5 minutes. Make a Béchamel sauce with the rest of the butter, the flour, and the milk. Add the artichoke mixture, and simmer gently for about 12 minutes. Rub through a sieve. Dilute with the white stock, and heat to boiling point, but do not boil. Season with salt and a pinch of white pepper. Just before serving, add the cream and the chervil.

Purée of Artichoke Soup

6 artichokes   *3 medium potatoes*
155 g (5½ oz) butter   *salt and pepper*
¾ litre (1¼ pints) chicken stock   *croûtons*
¾ litre (1¼ pints) hot water

Trim and wash the artichokes. Cut them in half vertically, and remove the chokes with a sharp knife. Melt 45 g (1½ oz) butter in a heavy pan, and add the artichokes. Stir with a wooden spoon until well mixed with the butter. Add hot water and chicken stock. Cover and simmer steadily for 1 hour. Add the potatoes, peeled and thickly sliced, and cook for a further 20 minutes. Remove from the fire, take out the artichokes, and scrape the fleshy bits from the leaves with a silver spoon (artichokes tend to discolour, but there would be less discoloration with silver). Discard the leaves, and add the fleshy scrapings to the pan. Mouli or blend this mixture, and return to the washed pan. Heat over a medium flame, and add more stock if the mixture is too thick. Correct the seasoning. Reduce heat, and add the remaining butter in small pieces. Tip the saucepan this way and that to blend the butter. Do not stir. Serve with croûtons.

Jerusalem Artichoke Soup

1 kg (2¼ lb) Jerusalem artichokes	*4 tablespoons cold milk*
	1 level tablespoon flour
85 g (3 oz) onions	*salt*
60 g (2 oz) butter	*sugar*
420 ml (¾ pint) boiled milk	*croûtons*
560 ml (1 pint) warm water	

Peel the artichokes, and cut into thin slices. Peel and slice the onions. Melt the butter in a soup pan, and add the sliced onions, and melt, but do not brown. Add the sliced artichokes and simmer for 15 minutes. Add the warm water, salt to taste, and a big pinch of sugar. Bring to the boil, cover, and simmer for about 20 minutes. Pour contents of pan into the bowl of an electric liquidizer, and blend to a purée. Return the mixture to the washed pan, add the boiled milk, and mix thoroughly with a wooden spoon. Blend the cold milk into the flour, and stir into the soup. Bring to the boil, stirring continuously for about 5 minutes. Serve very hot with fried croûtons.

Cream of Asparagus Soup

225 g (8 oz) green asparagus	*280 ml (½ pint) white stock*
60 g (2 oz) butter	*140 ml (¼ pint) cream*
1 tablespoon flour	*1 tablespoon chervil or parsley*
1 litre (1¾ pints) milk	

Use the tender tips of the asparagus only. Blanch them, cut them into 2½ cm (1 in) pieces, and cook them for about 10 minutes very gently in half the butter. Make a Béchamel sauce with the rest of the butter, the flour and the milk. Combine the partially cooked asparagus with the sauce, and simmer gently for 15 minutes. Add the white stock, and heat to boiling point. Season to taste, and just before serving, add the cream and the chervil or parsley.

Asparagus Velouté

1 kg (2¼ lb) asparagus	*1 litre (1¾ pints) white stock*
170 g (6 oz) butter	*3 egg yolks*
110 g (4 oz) flour	*140 ml (¼ pint) cream*

Blanch the tips of the asparagus, and simmer lightly in butter in a covered pan. Prepare Velouté sauce: blend the flour into 110 g (4 oz) melted butter. Stir over low heat, and gradually add hot white stock, stirring. When the mixture is thick and smooth, combine it with the asparagus mixture, and cook very gently, stirring from time to time, for about 15 minutes. Sieve, mouli or blend the mixture, reserving a few of the best asparagus tips for a garnish. Dilute as required with additional stock. Thicken with a liaison of yolks and cream, stirring. Do not boil after adding the liaison. At the last minute, add 60 g (2 oz) butter in small bits, tipping the pan to blend. Garnish with the asparagus tips.

Rich Aubergine Soup

1 finely chopped onion	*pinch of sugar*
1 clove garlic, minced	*1 bay leaf*
2 tablespoons minced meat	*¾ litre (1¼ pints) stock*
1 tablespoon finely chopped green pepper	*1 aubergine, peeled and diced*
1 tablespoon oil	*280 ml (½ pint) milk or cream*
1 tablespoon finely chopped, peeled and seeded tomato	

Fry onion, garlic, meat and green pepper in oil, then add remaining ingredients, except milk or cream. Season to taste and simmer until aubergine is tender. Just before serving, add milk or cream. Reheat and serve without boiling.

Cream of Barley Soup

250 g (9 oz) pearl barley   *1 litre (1¾ pints) white stock*
1 stalk celery   *140 ml (¼ pint) cream*

Wash the barley in several waters, then soak it for 1 hour in warm water. Drain it, and add it to the white stock. Add the chopped celery, and bring to the boil. Simmer gently for 2½ hours. Reserve 2 tablespoons of the cooked barley, and rub the rest of the mixture through a sieve. Return to the washed pan. Heat, and finish with the cream and the reserved barley.

Bean Soup

225 g (8 oz) dried haricot or   *2 large cloves garlic, chopped*
  butter beans, soaked overnight   *bunch parsley, chopped*
1 litre (1¾ pints) water   *salt, black pepper*
5 tablespoons olive oil

Simmer the beans in unsalted water until they are just cooked; not falling to pieces. Remove ¼ to ½ of the beans, reserving them. Blend or mouli the rest. Season well, and return the blended mixture to a clean pan. Dilute with water, if too thick. Reheat with the whole beans. In a separate pan, cook the garlic gently in 2 tablespoons of olive oil, until it just begins to turn golden. Add to the soup with the parsley and the remaining 3 tablespoons of oil. Serve very hot.

Broad Bean Soup

340 g (12 oz) shelled broad
    beans
1 small onion
45 g (1½ oz) butter
½ teaspoon chopped savory

1 litre (1¾ pints) chicken stock
½ teaspoon sugar
salt and freshly ground black
    pepper
70 ml (½ gill) double cream

Peel and chop the onion. Heat butter in saucepan, add onion and cook over low heat until onion is soft and transparent. Add stock, sugar, a pinch of salt and the savory, bring to the boil, add beans, and cook until tender. Remove and skin about a dozen beans for garnish, and purée the remainder. Put through a sieve, return the purée to a clean pan, heat through, season with salt and freshly ground black pepper and blend in the cream. Serve garnished with reserved skinned beans.

Cream of Bean Soup

450 g (1 lb) French beans
60 g (2 oz) butter
15 g (½ oz) flour
1 litre (1¾ pints) milk

280 ml (½ pint) white stock
140 ml (¼ pint) cream
1 tablespoon chervil

Blanch and refresh the beans, which have been topped and tailed, and cut into 2½ cm (1 in) lengths. Cook gently in half the butter for about 8 minutes. Make a Béchamel sauce with the rest of the butter, the flour and milk. Add the beans to this sauce, and simmer together very gently for about 12 minutes. Rub through a sieve. Place in the washed out soup pan, and dilute with the white stock. Heat to boiling point, and season to taste. Just before serving, stir in the cream and heat again, but do not boil. Sprinkle on the chervil, and serve very hot.

Bean Soup from Kenya

450 g (1 lb) dried black beans	*pinch oregano*
85 g (3 oz) chopped bacon	*pinch red pepper*
2 tablespoons oil	*salt and pepper*
1 crushed clove garlic	*stock*
1 chopped onion	

Soak beans for several hours. Cook until tender in unsalted water. Drain, reserving bean liquor. Brown bacon in oil, add onion, garlic and seasoning. Rub beans through a sieve, and combine with bacon mixture. Thin with bean liquor and stock until desired consistency is obtained. Season to taste.

West African Bean Soup

285 g (10 oz) dried butter or	*2 aubergines, peeled and*
haricot beans	*parboiled for 5 minutes*
2 large tomatoes, peeled and	*1 tablespoon oil*
seeded	*salt and chilli pepper to taste*
3 onions	*1 litre (1¾ pints) water*
	1 meat bone or bouillon cube

Soak beans for several hours. Chop onions. Fry onions and beans in oil, then add water and bone or cube. Simmer until beans are tender. Season, chop tomatoes and aubergines finely, and add to the soup. Serve very hot.

Potage à la Condé

450 g (1 lb) dried kidney beans	*280 ml (½ pint) red wine*
1 medium onion, studded with	*salt*
a clove	*bouquet garni*
1 carrot, quartered	*60 g (2 oz) butter*
60 g (2 oz) lean bacon	*croûtons*

Pick over and wash the beans, and cover them with cold water. Bring to the boil, then drain off the water. Add fresh water, bring to the boil, skim, and add the onion, the carrot quarters, the bouquet garni, and the bacon, cut into large dice, blanched and lightly fried. Boil the red wine and add to the beans. Simmer all together very gently, uncovered, until the beans are tender. Season. Remove the garnish, and drain the beans, reserving the liquor. Purée the beans in a blender or put through a mouli, and return to the washed pan with the bean liquor. If the mixture is too thick, add a little stock. Blend in 60 g (2 oz) butter at the last minute, and serve with tiny croûtons.

Potage Marguerite

225 g (8 oz) kidney beans	*1 dessertspoon tomato purée*
1 carrot	*60 g (2 oz) butter*
1 onion	*2 litres (3½ pints) water or*
1 turnip	*vegetable stock*
bouquet garni	*grated cheese*
4 tomatoes	*salt and pepper*

Soak the beans. Drain. Melt the butter in a soup pan, and add the diced carrot, onion and turnip and the beans. Toss over the heat for a few moments, then add the skinned and quartered tomatoes, the tomato purée, and the herbs. Pour on the water, and simmer until the beans are soft, but not falling to pieces (approximately 2 hours, but test often, as much depends on their age). Remove the herbs, season to taste, and serve with grated cheese.

Potage Soissonnaise

450 g (1 lb) dried haricot beans,	*60 g (2 oz) lean bacon*
soaked	*salt*
1 medium onion studded with a	*bouquet garni*
clove	*60 g (2 oz) butter*
1 carrot	*croûtons*

Pick over and wash the soaked beans, and put them into 2¼ litres (4 pints) cold water. Bring to the boil, skim, and add the onion, the quartered carrot, the bouquet garni, and the bacon, cut into large dice, blanched and lightly fried. Simmer all together, uncovered, until the beans are tender. Add salt to taste. Drain the beans, remove the garnish, and strain the liquor. Purée the beans in a blender or mouli, and put back into the washed pan with the bean liquor. Add a little stock if the mixture is too thick. Blend in the butter, and serve with croûtons.

Beet Soup

2 leeks	*1 large beetroot*
450 g (1 lb) potatoes	*110 g (4 oz) butter*
1⅛ litres (2 pints) white stock	*70 ml (½ gill) cream*

Wash the leeks and slice the white part, discarding the rest. Cook gently in 30 g (1 oz) butter until soft but not brown. Peel and quarter the potatoes, and add to the mixture. Add the stock, and cook at a good simmer, covered, until the potatoes are tender. Mouli, sieve, or blend the mixture, and return to the washed pan. Peel the beetroot and cut it into chunks. Bake it in the oven at moderate heat with 30 g (1 oz) butter and a pinch of salt until it is tender. Sieve, mouli, or blend it, and add to the potato purée. Dilute if necessary with additional stock, and at the last moment, stir in the rest of the butter and the cream.

Beetroot Soup

4 raw beetroots, scrubbed	*salt and pepper*
¾ litre (1¼ pints) white stock	*3 tablespoons*
1 chicken bouillon cube	*soured cream or yoghourt*
60 g (2 oz) butter	

Grate or shred the raw beetroots, and cook them in butter for 20 minutes. Heat the stock and cube to simmering point, and add gradually to the beetroot. Cook until the beetroot is soft, then simmer for a further ½ hour. Sieve or blend the soup. Place in a clean pan, season to taste, then reheat, and add the cream or yoghourt. Do not boil after adding the cream.

La Bisque aux Légumes

450 g (1 lb) lentils	*pepper*
3 leeks	*1 teaspoonful paprika*
3 carrots	*2¼ litres (4 pints) stock or*
a stick celery	*water*
2 egg yolks	*French bread*

Soak the lentils. Drain, and cover with the stock or water, and simmer for 2 hours with the sliced white part of the leeks, the sliced carrots and celery. Sieve or mouli the contents, or purée in an electric liquidizer. Return to the washed pan. Beat the yolks well in a small bowl, season them with paprika. Add a little hot soup to the yolks, then add the yolk mixture to the soup. Line each soup bowl with thin slices of French bread, which have been lightly toasted and rubbed with a cut clove of garlic. Serve hot, but take care not to boil after the addition of the yolks.

Borshch

1 onion	*1 dessertspoon vinegar*
1 parsnip	*1 tablespoon sugar*
1 carrot	*30 g (1 oz) lard*
1 large raw beetroot	*handful of bacon bones*
170 g (6 oz) shredded cabbage	*seasoning*
2 tablespoons tomato purée	*soured cream*
1 bay leaf	

Cook the bacon bones with 1¼ litres (2½ pints) water for stock. Bring to the boil, skim and simmer for 30 minutes. Melt lard in large saucepan. Chop vegetables (do not peel beetroot), and roughly fry them in lard for about 5 minutes. Pour on hot stock, strained. Add tomato purée and everything else (except cream). Simmer for 20 minutes. Strain, and serve hot with a dollop of soured cream for each serving.

Brussels Sprouts and Chestnut Purée

675 g (1½ lb) Brussels sprouts   *225 g (8 oz) unsweetened*
1¼ litres (2½ pints) chicken   *chestnut purée*
*   stock*   *2 tablespoons double cream*

Trim and wash the sprouts. Boil them in the chicken stock
until they are very soft. Put all through a sieve or blender.
Return to the clean pan, and blend in the chestnut purée.
Reboil and correct the seasoning. Away from the heat, stir
in the double cream.

Purée Flamande

450 g (1 lb) Brussels sprouts   *140 ml (¼ pint) milk*
4 medium potatoes   *seasoning*
60 g (2 oz) butter   *croûtons*
560 ml (1 pint) white stock

Trim and wash and lightly blanch sprouts, then refresh
them. Melt butter in a large pan and gently sweat sprouts.
Add peeled and sliced potatoes, and hot stock. Place lid on,
bring to a boil, and simmer for ¾ hour. Sieve or blend.
Return to a clean pan, add milk and adjust seasoning. If
required, add more stock for correct consistency. Serve with
fried croûtons.

Caboches in Potage (Early English Cabbage Soup)

1 large onion   *⅛ teaspoon ground cloves*
2 leeks   *⅛ teaspoon crushed saffron*
60 g (2 oz) butter   *   threads*
1⅛ litres (2 pints) chicken stock   *⅛ teaspoon mace*
1 small cabbage   *salt*

Trim, split, and well wash the leeks; cut into 5 cm (2 in)
pieces. In a skillet, sauté the minced onion and the leeks in
the butter over low heat until vegetables soften. Transfer
to a large saucepan and add the stock, the cabbage, cored

and cut into 8 wedges, and the cloves, saffron and mace. Season to taste with salt, bring to the boil, and simmer, covered, for 25 minutes, or until cabbage is tender. Serve very hot.

Savoy Cabbage Soup

1 medium Savoy cabbage	*140 ml (¼ pint) soured cream*
1 large onion	*parsley*
1⅛ litres (2 pints) brown stock	*caraway seeds*
30 g (1 oz) butter	

Blanch and shred the cabbage. Melt the butter in a large soup pan. Add the minced onion, and sweat in the butter. Add the cabbage and stock, and simmer all together, covered, for about 10 minutes. Correct the seasoning and serve in bowls, topping each serving with a dollop of soured cream, a sprinkling of parsley, and a couple of caraway seeds.

Soupe aux Choux

60 g (2 oz) butter	*1¼ litres (2½ pints) vegetable*
4 small onions	*stock*
1 clove garlic	*seasoning*
1 rasher bacon	*60 g (2 oz) French beans*
1 cabbage	*grated Parmesan cheese*
	toasted French bread

Blanch and coarsely chop the cabbage. Melt the butter in a large saucepan. Add chopped onions, crushed chopped garlic and chopped bacon. Sweat all gently. Add cabbage. Pour stock over and season. Bring gently to the boil. Simmer, covered, for 1½ hours. Add beans cut in 2½ cm (1 in) lengths. Cook a few minutes. Serve with toasted rounds of French bread on top, and hand round a bowl of Parmesan cheese.

Viennese Cabbage Soup

1 large cabbage
1⅛ litres (2 pints) white stock
1 tablespoon flour

6 skinless pork sausages
15 g (½ oz) butter
salt and pepper

Clean the cabbage and remove the tough outer leaves. Shred it finely. Melt the butter in a large soup pan and add the cabbage. Stir and cook until it just begins to brown. Sprinkle on the flour, mixing well, and cook until flour starts to brown. Heat the stock to boiling point, then pour slowly over the cabbage mixture, stirring. Season to taste. Reduce heat, and simmer gently for 1 hour. Fry the sausages. Slice and add to the soup just before serving.

Crème de Carottes

675 g (1½ lb) carrots
2 onions
1 clove garlic
1 potato
1 egg yolk
1 tablespoon flour

840 ml (1½ pints) milk
  and water mixed
70 ml (½ gill) cream
60 g (2 oz) butter
salt and black pepper
chopped parsley

Melt the butter in a soup pan. Add the finely sliced carrots and onions, and crushed garlic. Season with salt and pepper, and cook slowly with the lid on for 10 minutes, stirring occasionally. Add the peeled and sliced potato, and cook for another few minutes. Add the flour, and stir until smooth. Pour on the liquid, and stir over the heat until it comes to the boil. Simmer gently for 20 minutes. Strain or purée in the blender. Add the cream mixed into the yolk. Return to the pan and stir over the fire until it thickens, but do not boil. Sprinkle chopped parsley over, and serve.

Carrot and Watercress Soup

450 g (1 lb) carrots, sliced   *70 ml (½ gill) cream*
small bunch of watercress   *840 ml (1½ pints) white stock*
1 large onion   *seasoning*
45 g (1½ oz) butter   *croûtons*
1 tablespoon flour

Melt the butter in a soup pan. Put in the peeled and sliced carrots and onion and soften over low heat without browning. Sprinkle on the flour, stir well, and add the stock. Simmer until the carrots are tender. Rub through a sieve or blend, and return to the washed pan. Season to taste, and stir in the chopped leaves of watercress. Add the cream, and serve with croûtons.

Crécy Soup

225 g (8 oz) carrots, sliced   *¾ litre (1¼ pints) veal or*
1 medium onion, chopped   *   chicken stock*
30 g (1 oz) rice   *140 g (5 oz) butter*
1 sprig thyme   *croûtons*

Simmer carrots and onion in a covered pan with 60 g (2 oz) of the butter for about 10 minutes without browning. Add rice, stock and thyme, and cook gently for 20 to 30 minutes. Remove the thyme sprig, and sieve or blend the soup, adding stock, if necessary. Return to the clean pan, reheat, and just before serving, stir in 30 g (1 oz) butter. Fry the croûtons in the remaining butter, and serve with the soup.

Cauliflower Soup with Bread Dumplings

1¾ litres (3 pints) water   *60 g (2 oz) flour*
1 cauliflower   *salt*
60 g (2 oz) butter   *pinch of mace*

For Dumplings:
1 egg   *parsley*
85 g (3 oz) breadcrumbs   *a nut of butter*

Boil cleaned and trimmed cauliflower in salted water. When
nearly soft, remove from pot and separate into florets.
Thicken liquid with a roux of the butter and flour. Add
mace and cook for 20 minutes.

To make dumplings: moisten breadcrumbs with milk.
Cream butter, egg and salt. Add breadcrumbs and parsley.
Form into tiny dumplings, and drop these into the soup.
Boil for 3 to 5 minutes. Lastly, add the cauliflower florets.

Crème de Ma Grande Tante

1 cauliflower   *110 g (4 oz) butter*
1 litre (1¾ pints) stock   *4 egg yolks*
140 ml (¼ pint) milk   *salt*

Take off the outside leaves of the cauliflower, separate it
into florets, wash it thoroughly, and cook in lightly salted
water. When soft, drain it, and sieve or blend. Add this
purée to the stock, and bring it to the boil gradually over a
low fire. Simmer for about 15 minutes. Draw the saucepan
to the side of the stove, and add the milk. Taste for seasoning.
and if too salty, add a little milk. Add the butter, stirring.
Beat the yolks with a little water, and add them to the soup,
beating it gently. Beat until the yolks thicken the soup to
a cream, but on no account allow the mixture to boil.

Purée Du Barry

1 medium cauliflower   *60 g (2 oz) butter*
4 medium potatoes   *1 tablespoon chervil*
¾ litre (1¼ pints) milk, plus   *croûtons*
*   140 ml (¼ pint) milk*

Blanch and drain the cauliflower. Cook with the peeled and
sliced potatoes in ¾ litre (1¼ pints) milk for about 20 minutes,
gently. Season with salt and white pepper. Mouli, sieve or

blend the mixture. Return to the cleaned pan, and dilute with remaining milk. Heat and add the butter and the chervil. Serve hot with fried croûtons to garnish.

Cream of Celery Soup

2 bunches of celery
60 g (2 oz) butter
1 tablespoon flour
1 litre (1¾ pints) milk

140 ml (¼ pint) cream
280 ml (½ pint) white stock
1 tablespoon parsley

Trim, wash thoroughly, and blanch the celery. Cut it into 5 cm (2 in) chunks, and cook gently in half the butter for about 10 minutes. Make a Béchamel sauce with the remainder of the butter, flour, and the milk. Combine the sauce with the celery, and simmer gently for 15 minutes. Rub through a sieve. Return to the washed pan, and add the stock. Heat to boiling point, season to taste, and just before serving, add the cream. Serve very hot with a sprinkling of finely chopped parsley.

Dill Celery Soup

225 g (8 oz) chopped celery
110 g (4 oz) chopped onion
110 g (4 oz) diced potato
85 g (3 oz) butter

1⅛ litres (2 pints) chicken stock
1 teaspoon dill weed
2 tablespoons cream

Stew celery, onion and potato gently in the butter in a covered pan for 10 minutes, taking care that the vegetables do not brown. Add stock and dill weed (not dill seed). Simmer for 20 minutes if you have a liquidizer; 40 minutes if a mouli, then either liquidize or mouli the soup. Pour through a sieve into a clean pan. Bring slowly to simmering point, seasoning with salt, pepper and more dill weed, if required. Add the cream just before serving. Chopped fennel leaves can be substituted for the dill, if preferred.

Cheddar Cheese Soup with Vegetables

6 spring onions
60 g (2 oz) butter
3 tablespoons flour
840 ml (1½ pints) chicken stock
110 g (4 oz) diced celery
110 g (4 oz) diced carrot
salt and white pepper

310 g (11 oz) sharp Cheddar
   cheese, grated
140 ml (¼ pint) scalded milk
dash cayenne
4 slices streaky bacon
parsley

Melt the minced spring onions in the butter. Stir in the flour, and cook over a low heat, stirring, for 3 minutes. Remove pan from the heat, and add the hot chicken stock, whisking until the mixture is smooth. Add the celery, carrot and salt and pepper to taste, and cook over moderate heat for 20 minutes. Stir in the Cheddar cheese, the milk and a dash of cayenne, and cook, stirring, until the cheese is melted. Simmer the soup for an additional 5 minutes, and adjust the seasoning. Add a bit more milk, if desired. Sauté the diced bacon in a skillet until crisp, and drain on paper towels. Use the bacon to garnish the soup, along with a sprinkling of minced parsley.

Crème aux Marrons

1⅛ litres (2 pints) good chicken
   stock
560 ml (1 pint) cream

450 g (1 lb) peeled chestnuts
salt and pepper
2 tablespoons brandy

Simmer chestnuts in stock until quite soft. Strain. Measure remaining stock, and make up to 1⅛ litres (2 pints) with water. Bring back to boiling point and sieve chestnuts into liquid. Stir in cream, correct seasoning, add brandy, and re-heat carefully in a bain-marie.

Cream of Chicory Soup

450 g (*1 lb*) chicory
60 g (*2 oz*) butter
1 tablespoon flour
1 litre (*1¾ pints*) milk

280 ml (*½ pint*) white stock
140 ml (*¼ pint*) cream
1 tablespoon chopped chervil
   or parsley

Blanch, drain well, and chop the chicory. Cook in half the butter for 5 minutes. Make Béchamel sauce with the rest of the butter, the flour, and the milk. Combine the chicory and the sauce, and simmer gently for 15 minutes. Rub through a sieve. Place in the washed soup pan, and dilute with white stock. Heat to the boiling point, season to taste, and just before serving, stir in the cream. Heat again, but do not allow the mixture to boil. Sprinkle on the chervil or parsley.

Cob Nut (Filbert) Soup

45 g (*1½ oz*) melted butter
170 g (*6 oz*) chopped celery
170 g (*6 oz*) chopped onion
4 tablespoons wholewheat flour
½ teaspoon sea salt
black pepper

½ teaspoon tomato paste
420 ml (*¾ pint*) milk
420 ml (*¾ pint*) vegetable stock
85 g (*3 oz*) ground filberts
   (cob nuts)
85 g (*3 oz*) chopped filberts

Melt the butter in a pan, add the celery and onion, and sauté until soft. Stir in the flour, salt, tomato paste and freshly ground black pepper, then slowly add the milk, stock and ground nuts (finely minced or pounded in a mortar), and stir until blended. If mixture is too thick, thin with additional stock or milk. Simmer for 15 minutes, and serve with the chopped nuts.

Corn Chowder

110 g (4 oz) salt pork	*560 ml (1 pint) milk*
1 medium onion	*2 small tins whole kernel corn*
3 large ribs celery	*parsley*
½ green pepper	*paprika*
2 large potatoes	*salt*
45 g (1½ oz) flour	*bay leaf*

Melt the chopped salt pork in a large heavy pan. Add the chopped onion, the chopped celery and the chopped green pepper, and sauté until golden. Add the peeled and diced potatoes, 560 ml (1 pint) water, ½ teaspoon salt, ¼ teaspoon paprika, and bay leaf. Simmer, covered, until the potatoes are just tender. Blend 140 ml (¼ pint) of the cold milk into the flour, bring to the boil, and add to the soup. Then heat and add the remaining milk and the drained corn kernels. Heat, but do not boil, and serve with chopped parsley sprinkled on top.

Courgette Soup

1⅛ litres (2 pints) white stock	*15 g (½ oz) butter*
2 courgettes, thinly sliced	*2 tablespoons grated Parmesan*
110 g (4 oz) shaped noodles	*cheese*
or macaroni	

Bring stock to the boil, and add courgettes and pasta. Cook until tender, about 15 minutes. Add butter, swirl the pan and, just before removing from the heat, add grated cheese.

Potage Crème de Courgettes

450 g (1 lb) courgettes	*scant 280 ml (½ pint) white*
60 g (2 oz) butter	*stock*
1 tablespoon flour	*140 ml (¼ pint) cream*
1 litre (1¾ pints) milk	*1 tablespoon chervil*

Slice and blanch the courgettes. Drain, and cook gently in half the butter for 5 minutes. Make a Béchamel sauce with

the remaining butter, flour, and the milk. Add the courgettes, and simmer together gently for about 15 minutes.
Rub through a sieve or blend. Dilute with the white stock,
and heat to boiling point. Season to taste with salt and
white pepper. Add the cream just before serving, and heat
again, but do not boil. Sprinkle chopped chervil on top.

Garlic Soup with Egg

1 whole head garlic	*olive oil*
1⅛ litres (2 pints) chicken stock	*4 eggs*
4 tomatoes	*chopped parsley*

Pound the garlic in a mortar. Distribute it among four
earthenware soup bowls which can be put over direct heat,
with a good teaspoonful of olive oil in the bottom of each
bowl. Peel, seed and chop the tomatoes, and divide evenly
among the bowls of garlic and oil. Cook over gentle heat
for a few minutes until the tomatoes run juice. Then pour
over hot stock, filling each bowl two-thirds full. Simmer for
about 7 minutes. Break an egg into each bowl, and as soon
as the eggs are set, serve the soup with a little parsley
sprinkled on top of each serving.

Cream of Leek Soup

450 g (1 lb) leeks	*280 ml (½ pint) white stock*
60 g (2 oz) butter	*140 ml (¼ pint) cream*
1 tablespoon flour	*1 tablespoon chervil*
1 litre (1¾ pints) milk	

Wash the leeks, trim off the tough green ends, and shred.
Blanch, and drain well. Cook them for 10 minutes very
gently in 30 g (1 oz) butter. Do not brown. Make a Béchamel
sauce with the rest of the butter, the flour and the milk.
Combine the leeks and the sauce, and simmer together for

about 15 minutes. Rub through a sieve, and place in the washed pan. Dilute with the white stock, and heat to boiling point. Season to taste, stir in the cream, and heat again, but do not boil. Sprinkle on chervil and serve.

Leek and Pumpkin Soup

450 g (1 lb) pumpkin
225 g (8 oz) potatoes
1 Spanish onion
110 g (4 oz) fresh broad beans,
    peeled
560 ml (1 pint) milk
1 small leek

60 g (2 oz) butter
560 ml (1 pint) chicken stock
140 ml (¼ pint) double cream
110 g (4 oz) boiled rice
2 tablespoons chopped chervil
    or parsley
salt and cayenne pepper

Peel and dice the pumpkin and the potatoes. Chop the onion, and sauté in half the butter until golden. Add diced pumpkin and potatoes, beans and milk. Bring to the boil, and simmer for 45 minutes, stirring occasionally. Be careful that the mixture does not scorch. Strain through a sieve, or blend, and put back into the clean saucepan. Add salt and pepper to taste. Cut the leek into very thin slices, and melt in remaining butter. Add to the soup, along with the hot chicken stock, and bring slowly to the boil. Simmer for 10 minutes. Stir in cream, boiled rice, and chopped parsley or chervil, and serve very hot.

Lentil Soup

250 g (9 oz) red lentils
2 medium onions
2 leeks

30 g (1 oz) butter
salt and pepper
1 litre (1¾ pints) water or stock

Slice the onions and leeks, and fry lightly in butter. Add lentils, mix well, then add water or stock and seasoning. Simmer until lentils are very soft, about 30 to 45 minutes. Liquidize or put through a sieve. Reheat, correct seasoning, and serve with croûtons.

Green Lentil and Watercress Soup

110 g (4 oz) green lentils   *60 g (2 oz) butter*
small bunch watercress

Trim the watercress, reserving a few of the best leaves as garnish. Soak the lentils for 2 hours, drain and place in a saucepan with 1½ litres (2½ pints) water. Simmer without salt until the lentils are tender, about 35 to 45 minutes. Wash, chop and soften the watercress in half the butter. Combine with the lentils, and sieve the entire mixture into a clean pan. Season, and if too thick, add more stock or water. Swirl in the remainder of the butter just before serving. Serve very hot, sprinkled with the watercress leaves.

Purée of Lentil Soup à la Conti

400 g (14 oz) lentils   *bouquet garni*
1 medium onion   *60 g (2 oz) lean bacon*
1 carrot   *60 g (2 oz) butter*
1 clove   *croûtons*

Wash and pick over the lentils. Add them to 1¾ litres (3 pints) cold water. Bring to the boil, skim, add the onion studded with the clove, the quartered carrot, bouquet garni, and the diced, blanched and lightly fried bacon. Simmer very gently, uncovered, until the lentils are done, about 35 to 45 minutes. Season to taste, drain, reserving the cooking liquor, and remove the garnishes. Put the lentils through a sieve or mouli, and return to the clean pan together with the liquor. Bring to the boil and blend in the butter. Serve with buttered croûtons.

Potage de Crème de Laitue

2 large heads of lettuce (Cos, if
  available)
60 g (2 oz) onion, finely
  chopped
30 g (1 oz) butter
¾ litre (1¼ pints) milk

22 g (¾ oz) flour
salt and pepper
1 teaspoon arrowroot
70 ml (½ gill) cream
borage

Finely shred the lettuce, melt the butter in a large pan, and
add the onion. Sweat gently for several minutes, then add
the lettuce. Cover and simmer gently 5 to 7 minutes, draw
the pan aside, and add the flour. Mix well. Bring the milk
to the boil, then add it and adjust the seasoning. Simmer
very gently 15 to 20 minutes, then sieve or blend. Return
to the clean pan, and add the liaison: 1 teaspoon arrowroot
mixed smoothly into the cream. Bring to the boiling point,
but do not boil. Serve with chopped borage sprinkled on
top.

Minestrone Soup

225 g (8 oz) dried kidney or
  haricot beans
225 g (8 oz) salt pork
2 cloves garlic
1 Spanish onion
2¼ litres (4 pints) beef stock
4 carrots
4 stalks celery
½ small head cabbage
4 sprigs curly endive

4 large tomatoes
225 g (8 oz) green beans
110 g (4 oz) frozen peas
170 g (6 oz) macaroni in 5 cm
  (2 in) lengths
2 tablespoons chopped parsley
2 tablespoons olive oil
4 tablespoons Parmesan cheese
salt and pepper

Soak the beans for several hours. Drain, and simmer them
in unsalted water to cover until just tender. Dice salt pork,
and sauté in a frying-pan until golden. Finely chop garlic, cut
onion into quarters, and sauté with pork until golden. Add
beef stock, and simmer gently with finely-sliced carrots and
celery. Slice cabbage, endive; skin, seed and chop tomatoes.
Cut green beans into 2½ cm (1 in) lengths. Add all the

vegetables except the peas, bring to the boil, cover, and simmer very gently for about an hour. Twenty minutes before serving, add peas and macaroni, bring back to the boil, and simmer until macaroni is tender. If soup is too thick, add some water. Add salt and pepper to taste, and at the last minute, finely-chopped parsley and olive oil. Serve very hot with grated Parmesan cheese sprinkled on top.

Chinese Mushroom Soup

*225 g (8 oz) flat dark
    mushrooms
1 medium-sized onion
1 litre (1¾ pints) strong
    chicken stock*

*30 g (1 oz) butter
spring onions, or watercress
1 dessertspoon arrowroot*

Wash the mushrooms, and cut stalks level with caps. Chop these trimmings finely and slice the mushrooms. Slice the onion, and soften it in the butter. Add the mushrooms. Shake over the heat for 4 to 5 minutes, then add the stock and the arrowroot, slaked in a spoonful of cold water. Boil up and adjust the seasoning. A handful of sliced spring onions improves the soup, or half a bunch of coarsely chopped watercress, added just before the addition of arrowroot.

Oatmeal Soup

*1¾ litres (3 pints) stock or
    water
2 tablespoons diced root
    vegetables
2 tablespoons grated cheese*

*4 tablespoons oatmeal
pinch mace
280 ml (½ pint) milk
salt*

Clean vegetables and cut into dice. Cover oatmeal and vegetables with water or stock, bring to the boil, and simmer for about 30 minutes. Sieve and dilute with water or stock if necessary. Add salt and a pinch of mace. Stir in scalded milk, and heat to boiling point. Serve with grated cheese sprinkled on top.

Soupe à l'Oignon

60 g (2 oz) butter
6 onions
½ teaspoonful made mustard
salt and pepper
1 teaspoonful flour

140 ml (¼ pint) white wine
840 ml (1½ pints) brown stock
  or water
6 slices French bread
60 g (2 oz) Parmesan cheese

Melt the butter in an earthenware casserole. Slice the onions (which should be large; preferably purple French ones) finely, and add with salt and pepper and mustard. Brown very slowly over a low fire. This should take about 30 minutes. Add the flour, and stir until smooth. Add wine and stock or water, and bring slowly to the boil, stirring all the time. Draw aside, and leave to simmer for 25 minutes. In the bottom of the serving bowl or bowls, place a few thin slices of French bread and a sprinkling of cheese. Add salt and pepper, and pour on the hot soup. Sprinkle the top with the rest of the grated cheese, and glaze briefly under the grill.

Curried Parsnip Soup

85 g (3 oz) butter
1 large parsnip
110 g (4 oz) chopped onion
1 clove garlic, crushed
1 tablespoon flour

1 rounded teaspoon curry powder
1¾ litres (2 pints) hot beef stock
280 ml (½ pint) cream
chives

Peel and slice the parsnip. Put the onion, parsnip and garlic into a heavy pan with the butter and cook for 10 minutes slowly with the lid on. The vegetables must not brown, but sweat in the butter. Add flour and curry powder and stir well. Gradually add the hot beef stock, bring to the boil, then simmer until the parsnip is cooked. Blend or liquidize, and return to the cleaned pan. Adjust seasoning with salt, pepper and a pinch more curry powder, if needed. Add the cream and a sprinkling of chopped chives. Serve with croûtons.

Pasta e Patate

5 potatoes
1 small tin peeled tomatoes
  (225 g/8 oz)
1 onion
1⅛ litres (2 pints) beef stock

handful macaroni
oil
salt and pepper
Parmesan cheese

Cook the sliced onion gently in the oil until it is just turning golden. Add the peeled and cubed potatoes, the tomatoes and salt and pepper. Simmer, covered, for 15 minutes. Add the beef stock and cook for 5 minutes. Add the macaroni, and simmer until it is just cooked. Serve very hot sprinkled with Parmesan cheese.

Pea Soup with Frankfurters

1¾ litres (3 pints) water
85 g (3 oz) dried peas or lentils
30 g (1 oz) fat
30 g (1 oz) flour
½ onion

1 cooked frankfurter
1 clove garlic
pinch paprika
salt

Soak peas or lentils. Cook in the soaking water until soft, then force through a sieve. Make a light roux with the fat and flour. Pour the purée over, stir well, and simmer for 15 minutes. Add grated onion, crushed garlic, salt and a pinch of paprika. Cook gently for an additional 15 minutes, and just before serving add frankfurter cut into rounds.

Potage Saint-Germain

1 kg (2¼ lb) fresh peas
1 carrot
1 onion
1 clove garlic
840 ml (1½ pints) stock
chopped parsley

1 tablespoon flour
1 potato
140 ml (¼ pint) double cream
125 g (4½ oz) butter
croûtons

Melt 60 g (2 oz) butter in a soup pan. Chop the onion finely and the carrot and garlic, and add to the pan with the chopped shells of the peas. Season well with salt and pepper, and cook for 6 minutes with the lid on. Add the finely sliced, peeled potato, the flour, and three-quarters of the shelled peas. Add a little seasoning, and pour on the stock. Stir over the fire until it comes to the boil. Draw aside and simmer gently until all the vegetables are tender. Rub through a sieve, or purée in the blender, and return to the washed pan. Place on a slow fire, and slowly beat in 65 g (2½ oz) butter. Remove from the fire, and beat in three-quarters of the whipped cream. Cook the peas which are left until just tender, and add with the remainder of the whipped cream and parsley. Serve with croûtons.

Purée of Split Pea Soup

340 g (12 oz) split peas	*2 leeks*
60 g (2 oz) lean bacon	*60 g (2 oz) butter*
1 small carrot	*chervil*
1 small onion	*croûtons*

Pick over and wash split peas. Soak them in cold water for 2 hours, then drain, and cover with fresh cold water. Bring to the boil, skim, season, add a mirepoix of diced bacon, blanched and lightly fried in butter, and mixed with diced carrot and onion. Put in a bouquet garni and the white part of two leeks. When the peas are tender, discard the bouquet, blend or mouli, and return the purée to the clean pan. Finish with butter and a tablespoon of chervil leaves. Serve very hot with croûtons.

La Soupe au Pistou

1 tablespoon olive oil	*1 medium-sized courgette, diced*
1 purple French onion	
2 skinned, chopped and seeded tomatoes	*3 medium potatoes, peeled and diced*
1⅛ litres (2 pints) water	*2 chopped leeks*
225 g (8 oz) French beans, cut into 2½ cm (1 in) lengths	*60 g (2 oz) large vermicelli*
	3 garlic cloves
110 g (4 oz) haricot beans, cooked, but only just	*10 sprigs fresh basil*
	2 or 3 tablespoons olive oil
	Parmesan cheese

Melt the chopped onion in the oil. Add the tomatoes, and cook for a few minutes, then pour on the water. Season. When the water boils, throw in the green beans, the haricot beans, the courgette, the potatoes, and the leeks. Simmer gently for 10 minutes, then add the vermicelli in short lengths. Simmer until vermicelli is cooked. While the soup simmers, make the final addition: pound the garlic in a mortar with the basil leaves. When they are a paste, add the oil, drop by drop, as if making mayonnaise. Add this mixture to the soup at the very last minute off the fire, and serve with grated Parmesan cheese.

Minestra di Patate e Sedano

1 onion	*salt and pepper*
1 bunch celery	*2 tablespoons oil*
4 medium potatoes	*Parmesan cheese*
handful of rice	

Lightly brown the chopped onion in the oil. Add the potatoes cut into cubes, and season with salt and pepper. Cover with water, bring to the boil, and add the sliced celery. Simmer for ¾ hour, add the rice, and simmer for an additional 12 minutes. Serve with a bowl of grated Parmesan cheese.

Purée of Potato Soup Parmentier

2 leeks	*70 ml (½ gill) cream*
60 g (2 oz) butter	*chervil*
450 g (1 lb) potatoes	*1⅛ litres (2 pints) water*
2 white stock cubes	

Shred the white part of the leeks and sweat in 30 g (1 oz) butter. When soft but not brown, add the potatoes, peeled and quartered. Moisten with white stock made from the water and cubes. Add a little salt and pepper, and simmer until the potatoes are tender. Blend the mixture in an electric liquidizer, or sieve or mouli. Return to the washed pan. Add the cream, and finish off with 30 g (1 oz) butter and a tablespoon chervil. Serve very hot with croûtons, if desired.

Spicy Potato Soup

30 g (1 oz) butter	*1 tablespoon curry powder*
340 g (12 oz) stewing steak, coarsely chopped	*1 bay leaf*
2 chopped onions	*2 big potatoes, peeled and sliced*
1 litre (1¾ pints) water or stock	*1 dessertspoon vinegar*
salt and pepper	*cream*

Fry beef and onions in butter, add curry powder and continue frying a few minutes longer for the curry powder to lose its raw taste. Now add water or stock, and bay leaf; season and simmer about 45 minutes. Add potatoes and vinegar. Continue cooking until meat and potatoes are tender. Check seasoning, and remove bay leaf. A little cream may be added before serving.

Sweet Potato Soup

5 sweet potatoes
840 ml (1½ pints) white or
  brown stock

60 g (2 oz) butter
croûtons

Peel and quarter the sweet potatoes, and cook until tender in 560 ml (1 pint) stock. Sieve or blend the mixture, and return to the clean pan. Add the rest of the stock, bring to the boil, and finally incorporate the butter. Serve with tiny croûtons.

Pumpkin Soup

450 g (1 lb) pumpkin
1 sliced onion
1¾ litres (3 pints) salted
  water
420 ml (¾ pint) milk

2 tablespoons cream
salt and pepper
2 eggs
15 g (½ oz) butter

Peel pumpkin, and cut into pieces. Put it into a heavy saucepan with the onion and salted water. Cover and boil for 15 minutes, or until pumpkin is soft. Drain. Reserve the liquid, and sieve or blend the pumpkin. Put the puréed pumpkin into a bain-marie. Stir in the milk and cream. The soup should be the consistency of thin cream. Thin, if necessary, with reserved liquid. Season and cook over simmering water for 20 minutes. Beat the eggs. Add 2 table-spoons of soup to the mixture, and mix well. Gradually add this to the soup, stirring, until smooth and slightly thickened. Do not boil. Check for seasoning. Stir in the butter, and serve.

Rasam

The word 'mulligatawny', meaning 'pepper-water', derives from the Tamil word in South Indian cookery. (See Mulli-gatawny Soup, English-Style, p. 45) An aromatic meatless broth, it is known in South India as Rasam.

½ teaspoon black peppercorns
2½ cm (*1 in*) ball tamarind
   pulp
2 teaspoons Toor dhal
¼ teaspoon turmeric powder
½ teaspoon asafoetida powder

¼ teaspoon cumin seed
½ teaspoon mustard seed
1½ teaspoons salt
2 tomatoes
olive oil

Heat a little oil in a pan and lightly fry the peppercorns, Toor dhal, and asafoetida, then pound them well in a mortar. Heat some more oil, fry the mustard seed, and when it stops spitting, add one peeled, seeded and chopped tomato and the cumin seed. Cook for a few minutes, and reserve. Put the tamarind pulp into ¾ litre (1¼ pint) water, and soak for several minutes. Stir well, then squeeze out the pulp and discard it. Strain the remaining water into a saucepan and bring to the boil, adding the other tomato, peeled, but left whole, salt, the ground spices, and another 280 ml (½ pint) water. When it comes to the boil, add the fried mustard seed and the tomato mixture. A little more ground pepper may be added to make it really fiery. Serve hot in bowls with fried poppadum.

Cream of Rice Soup

225 g (*8 oz*) rice
560 ml (*1 pint*) white
   vegetable stock

280 ml (*½ pint*) cream
15 g (*½ oz*) butter
croûtons

Blanch and drain the rice. Simmer it very gently with the white stock and butter for about 45 minutes, covered. Sieve or mouli the mixture, and replace in the clean pan. Add the cream and heat again, but do not boil. Garnish, if desired, with tiny croûtons.

Shallots and Cheese Soup

4 slices white bread
75 g (2½ oz) butter
4 tablespoons grated Gruyère
  cheese
4 shallots

1 teaspoon flour
420 ml (¾ pint) stock
2 tablespoons cream
salt and pepper

Lightly brown each slice of bread in half the butter. Put the toasted bread in a soup tureen, sprinkle with 1 tablespoon grated cheese for each slice, and keep warm. Cook the sliced shallots in the rest of the butter. Add the flour, stir until blended, then add the hot stock. Cook, covered, over very low heat for ½ hour. Correct the seasoning with salt and pepper. Strain, and add the cream. Pour over the bread and cheese in the tureen, and serve.

Cream of Tomato Soup

450 g (1 lb) tomatoes
30 g (1 oz) butter
30 g (1 oz) flour
1 kg (2¼ lb) veal bones
3 onions
1 turnip
2 celery stalks

1 teaspoon sugar
15 g (½ oz) peppercorns
mixed herbs
salt and pepper
water
1 tablespoon lemon juice

Simmer the veal bones in 1¾ litres (3 pints) water for 2 hours, skimming. Add sliced turnip, celery and 2 onions, peppercorns and 1 teaspoon salt, and simmer for another hour. Strain the stock into a saucepan, and add tomatoes, 1 onion, and herbs, and simmer for 40 minutes. Sieve, and thicken with butter and flour blended. Add sugar, lemon juice, salt and pepper to taste. Heat gently, stirring, until the soup is creamy and hot.

Crème de Tomates et de Pommes de Terre

2 leeks	*salt*
225 g (8 oz) tomatoes	*3 sugar lumps*
340 g (12 oz) potatoes	*parsley or chervil*
45 g (1½ oz) butter	*70 ml (½ gill) cream*

Melt the butter in a heavy pan, and before it has bubbled, put in the white part of the leeks, well washed, and finely sliced. Let them just soften, not brown, in the butter. Add the peeled, seeded and chopped tomatoes, and let them cook until they exude juice. Add the peeled and diced potatoes, a seasoning of salt, and 3 sugar lumps. Cover with 840 ml (1½ pints) water. Bring to the boil, and simmer steadily for 30 minutes. Sieve or mouli the mixture, or blend in an electric liquidizer. Return to the washed pan, and when hot, add the cream. Just before serving, stir in a little finely chopped chervil or parsley.

Purée de Navets à la Freneuse

450 g (1 lb) small white turnips	*840 ml (1½ pints) white stock*
450 g (1 lb) potatoes	*60 g (2 oz) butter*

Peel, slice and blanch the turnips. Cook them gently in butter in a covered pan. Moisten with 280 ml (½ pint) stock, and cook slowly until three-quarters done. Add the peeled and sliced potatoes and the rest of the stock, and finish cooking at a fast simmer. Mouli, sieve or blend. Return to the clean pan, heat to the boiling point, and swirl in the butter.

Vegetable Chowder

1 lettuce	*1 medium carrot*
1 stalk celery	*60 g (2 oz) butter*
1 medium onion	*110 g (4 oz) noodles*

Remove the outer leaves of lettuce, and shred the rest. Wash and chop the celery, and chop the onion and the carrot.

Melt the butter in a heavy saucepan. Add the vegetables and simmer them for about 10 minutes. Add 560 ml (1 pint) boiling water. Bring again to the boil, and add the noodles. Simmer, covered, for 30 minutes, adding more water if the mixture is too thick. Correct the seasoning.

Ginger Vegetable Soup

1 litre (1¾ pints) stock
2 pieces fresh ginger, peeled
salt and pepper
½ small cauliflower

2 carrots, scraped
1 small head of celery
1 leek
4 tablespoons cream

Cook the ginger in stock until very tender, then rub through a sieve. Clean the vegetables, cut into small pieces or julienne. Add to the soup, season to taste and simmer until vegetables are just tender. Just before serving, add cream. A little ground ginger may be sprinkled over the soup before serving.

Peanut Vegetable Soup

250 g (9 oz) skinned and
 ground peanuts
1 chopped onion
1 stick celery, cut into pieces
¾ litre (1¼ pints) stock

280 ml (½ pint) milk
1 tablespoon flour
15 g (½ oz) butter
4 tablespoons cream
salt and pepper

Combine nuts, onion, celery and milk. Simmer for 1 hour, then rub through a sieve or liquidize. Make a sauce with butter, flour and stock. Add nut-vegetable mixture, bring to the boil again, check seasoning, and just before serving, add cream. If liked, sprinkle some coarsely ground roasted peanuts on top.

Pineapple Vegetable Soup

1 leek, chopped
1 tablespoon chopped parsley
30 g (1 oz) butter
140 ml (¼ pint) mashed,
   cooked pumpkin or pawpaw
420 ml (¾ pint) stock

1 pineapple, peeled and crushed
   or chopped finely
280 ml (½ pint) milk
salt and pepper
paprika
spring onions, chopped

Cook leek and parsley in butter until soft. Add pumpkin or pawpaw, pineapple, milk and stock. Season to taste. Bring to the boil, beating vigorously. Simmer for 15 minutes. Serve sprinkled with spring onions and paprika.

Potage aux Herbes

110 g (4 oz) sorrel
15 g (½ oz) lard
15 g (½ oz) butter
1¼ litres (2½ pints) stock
1 small heart lettuce

1 tablespoon chervil
2 egg yolks
1 teaspoon sugar
croûtons

Cut the sorrel and lettuce into strips. Chop the chervil. Melt the lard in a soup pan and add the sorrel, lettuce and chervil. Simmer, uncovered, for 10 minutes, stirring with a wooden spoon. Sprinkle on the sugar. Add the stock, cover the pan, and simmer for 30 minutes. Mix the egg yolks with a little cold stock. Remove soup from the fire, and add a cupful of the warm soup gradually to the egg mixture. Then add the mixture to the pan. Cut the butter into small pieces and add to the soup, swirling the pan to blend it in. Re-heat gently, but do not boil. Serve with croûtons handed separately.

Potage Bonne Femme

450 g (1 lb) potatoes	*3 sugar lumps*
3 carrots	*salt*
2 large leeks	*140 ml (¼ pint) cream*
45 g (1½ oz) butter	*parsley or chervil*
1⅛ litres (2 pints) water	

Melt the butter in a heavy soup pan. Put in the cleaned and finely-sliced leeks and the diced carrots. Let them get hot through and saturated with butter. Add the peeled and diced potatoes, the water, a little salt, and 3 lumps sugar. Cook steadily but not furiously for 30 minutes. Sieve or blend. Taste for seasoning, and when ready to serve, add the cream and finely-chopped parsley or chervil.

Potage de Flandres

4 potatoes	*½ teaspoon thyme*
2 sticks celery	*croûtons*
1 small tin tomato purée	*1 tablespoon chopped chervil*
2 small onions	*salt and pepper*
1 clove garlic	*1¾ litres (3 pints) water*
15 g (½ oz) butter	

Chop the peeled potatoes, celery, onions, garlic, and put into a soup pan with the water. Stir in the tomato purée. Add thyme, salt and pepper, and bring to the boil. Place over low heat and simmer for about 3 hours, giving an occasional stir with a wooden spoon. Strain off the liquid, and either mouli or blend the vegetables. Reserve the liquid, and add enough of it to the purée to make a creamy thick soup. Re-heat, add butter and chopped chervil, and serve with croûtons.

Potage Fermière

3 carrots	*60 g (2 oz) butter*
1 turnip	*110 g (4 oz) haricot beans*
2 leeks	*1⅛ litres (2 pints) white stock*
1 onion	*70 ml (½ gill) cream*
1 small cabbage heart	*chervil*

Soak the beans for 2 hours in cold water. Drain, and replace with fresh cold water. Bring slowly to the boil, and cook until tender. Reserve beans and bean liquor. Shred the carrots and the turnip. Clean and slice the white part of the leeks. Chop the onion, and shred the cabbage heart. Sweat these vegetables in the butter. Season and add the water in which the beans were cooked, and the stock. Cook gently, covered, for about an hour. Just before serving, add the reserved beans, the cream, and a sprinkling of chervil.

Potage Solférino

2 leeks	*small garlic clove*
2 carrots	*1⅛ litres (2 pints) white stock*
4 medium tomatoes	*225 g (8 oz) potatoes*
bouquet garni	*85 g (3 oz) butter*

Garnish:

2 potatoes	*chervil*
280 ml (½ pint) white stock	

Sweat in butter the sliced white part of the washed leeks, and the shredded, peeled carrots. Add the peeled, seeded and chopped tomatoes, a small bouquet garni, and the mashed clove of garlic. Cook gently for 10 minutes. Add the stock and the peeled and sliced potatoes. Season and simmer gently, covered, until vegetables are tender. Remove the bouquet garni, sieve or blend or mouli the mixture, and return to the clean pan. Bring to the boil, skim, and add butter. Garnish with small potato balls which have been scooped out with a vegetable baller and cooked until barely tender in white stock. Sprinkle chervil leaves on top.

Potage Véronique

450 g (1 lb) tomatoes
1 tablespoon tomato purée
2 onions
1 clove garlic
1 bay leaf
4 bruised peppercorns

60 g (2 oz) butter
1 tablespoon rice
840 ml (1½ pints) stock
chopped parsley
1 teaspoon caster sugar
salt and pepper

Melt the butter in a soup pan. Slice the onions and melt in the butter. Roughly cut up three-quarters of the tomatoes, and add to the pan, along with the tomato purée, bay leaf, clove of garlic, and peppercorns. Add a little salt. Cover the pan and cook slowly for 10 minutes, stirring occasionally. Rub through a sieve, and combine in the clean pan with the stock. Stir over the fire until it boils. Add the rice, previously cooked for 5 minutes in boiling salted water, and simmer the mixture for 15 minutes. Skin the remaining tomatoes, remove seeds, and cut into shreds. Add to the soup with the chopped parsley and sugar. Heat, but do not boil. Serve very hot with Mornay toast.

Mornay toast: cut day-old bread into wafer-thin slices, remove crusts, and lay on a baking sheet. Sprinkle well with Parmesan cheese, dust with paprika and cayenne, and brown in a slow oven.

Village Soup

450 g (1 lb) onions
1 head celery
1 egg yolk
lemon juice

2 tablespoons oil
salt
water

Cook the peeled and sliced onions in salted water until soft. Strain and purée. Add chopped celery, oil, and a little of the onion water, and bring to the boil. Beat the yolk and dilute it with a bit of the soup. Add this mixture to the rest of the soup, along with a squeeze of lemon juice. Heat, but do not boil.

Cream of Watercress Soup

1 bunch watercress
60 g (2 oz) butter
1 tablespoon flour
1 litre (1¾ pints) milk

280 ml (½ pint) white stock
140 ml (¼ pint) cream
1 tablespoon chervil

Blanch, press, and chop the watercress. Cook gently in half the butter for 5 minutes. Make a Béchamel sauce with the rest of the butter, the flour and the milk. Add the watercress mixture, and simmer together for 15 minutes, very gently. Rub through a sieve, mouli or blend. Dilute the mixture with the white stock, and heat to boiling point. Season to taste, and at the last minute stir in the cream and sprinkle on the chervil.

Potage Cressonnière

75 g (2½ oz) butter
2 onions
clove garlic
5 potatoes
bunch of watercress

840 ml (1½ pints) milk and
    water mixed
2 egg yolks
140 ml (1 gill) cream
2 slices stale bread
salt and black pepper

Melt the butter in a soup pan. Finely slice the onions and add with the chopped clove of garlic. Cook very slowly for 3 minutes without browning. Add the potatoes, cut into thin slices. Season with salt and freshly ground black pepper. Cover with the lid and cook very slowly for 10 minutes. Add half the roughly cut-up watercress. Leave for a little longer, and then pour on the liquid. Stir over the heat until it comes to the boil, then draw aside and leave to simmer for 15 minutes. Rub through a coarse wire sieve, or blend. Return to the clean pan with the yolks of egg mixed into the cream. Stir over a slow heat until it thickens without boiling. Scatter over the top the whole leaves of the rest of the bunch of watercress. Serve with fingers of dried toast.

Watercress and Bean Soup

1 small bunch watercress
5 lettuce leaves
30 g (1 oz) butter
280 ml (½ pint) white stock

110 g (4 oz) dried haricot
  beans, soaked overnight
140 ml (½ pint) cream

Cut off the thick end stalks from the watercress, and reserve a handful of the best leaves for garnish. Soak the beans for several hours. Simmer them in 1½ litres (2½ pints) unsalted water until soft but not falling apart. Melt the lettuce leaves and the trimmed watercress in the butter in a covered pan. Add the stock, and simmer for 10 minutes. Drain and sieve the beans, reserving the liquid. Sieve the watercress mixture into a clean pan. Add the sieved beans to the soup, and thin to the desired consistency with the bean liquor. Season, heat, slowly stir in the boiled cream. Do not re-boil once the cream has been added. Sprinkle reserved watercress leaves on top.

Yeast Soup

1¾ litres (3 pints) water
85 g (3 oz) bakers' yeast
60 g (2 oz) plain flour
parsley

Pasta:
1 egg
3 tablespoons milk

small pieces of carrot, celeriac,
  parsley root and onion
salt
60 g (2 oz) butter

85 g (3 oz) fine semolina
salt

Fry onion and yeast in butter. When yeast begins to brown at the edges, sprinkle on the flour, mix and pour on the water. Add finely chopped vegetables. Season with salt, whisk well, and cook for 20 minutes. Now prepare the pasta: beat the egg in a little milk, add semolina a little at a time, and salt. Using a teaspoon, drop small pieces of dough into the soup, and cook for about 5 minutes more.

Zuppa di Verdura

2 leeks	a handful of parsley
1 large onion	2 bunches of watercress
2 cloves of garlic	1 small packet of frozen
840 ml (1½ pints) chicken	spinach (225 g/8 oz)
stock	salt and pepper

Trim, wash and slice the leeks, including the green part.
Chop the onion and the garlic cloves. Boil all together in
the chicken stock, adding the parsley and watercress when
the onions and leeks are soft. Add the spinach, and stir all
together until well blended. Season with salt and pepper,
and pass through a sieve or blend. Re-heat in a clean pan,
adding a knob of butter.

CHAPTER EIGHT

Summer Soups

IN 1910, WHEN THE ROOF garden was opened at the old
Ritz-Carlton Hotel on New York's Madison Avenue, chef
Louis Diat presented Manhattan society with a new soup.
It was called Crème Vichyssoise Glacée, and it caused a
sensation in America. Vegetable soups had always been
hot, and someone had finally demonstrated that they are, if
anything, better cold. The invention was instrumental in
the downfall of jellied consommé, and hardly anybody
mourned its passing. Vichyssoise was based on the simple
leek and potato soup made by Diat's *maman* in the French
countryside, cooled for breakfast on warm days by the
addition of cold milk. The new soup was named after the
famous Vichy spa not far from the Diat's Borbonnais home,
as a fitting tribute to the fine cooking of the region.

Today, chilled soup is accepted as the perfect starter for
a luncheon or supper menu on a summer's day. It refreshes
the palate and stimulates the appetite; it is pretty to look at
and delicious to eat, and as it must be made ahead of time,
it liberates the cook. Summer soups can be made from most
summer vegetable crops, and at a time when these vege-

tables are both cheap and plentiful. Citrus fruits are useful adjuncts. Fresh orange juice makes ambrosia of a cold carrot soup, and lemons combine admirably with eggs and cream in the delectable Greek Avgolemono. The fruit soups widely served in Scandanavia are delicious served cold. Chilled seafood soups can be made from haddock or prawns combined with yoghourt; only the seafood need be cooked.

Summer soups abound, but perhaps the most spectacular is the classic Spanish Gazpacho, adorned with colourful side dishes of cucumber, slivered tomatoes, spring onions, green peppers and croûtons. There are many versions of Gazpacho, but the one on page 132 is my favourite.

Apple Soup

450 g (1 lb) cooking apples	*1 or 2 tablespoons cornflour*
2 tablespoons sugar	*15 g (½ oz) butter*
2 litres (3½ pints) water	*140 ml (¼ pint) white wine*
225 g (8 oz) sultanas	*1 lemon*
225 g (8 oz) currants	

Skin, core, and chop the apples, and put into a pan with the wine. Grate lemon rind over. Cook slowly until apples are soft, then press through a sieve. Return sieved mixture to a clean pan. Add water, sugar, currants and sultanas. Simmer gently for 30 minutes. Melt the butter in a small thick pan. Stir in the cornflour, and add this mixture gradually to the soup, stirring constantly. Simmer for another 10 minutes. Serve hot or cold.

Curried Apple Soup

75 g (2½ oz) butter	*1 Spanish onion*
560 ml (1 pint) chicken stock	*1 level tablespoon curry powder*
1 tablespoon cornflour	*140 ml (¼ pint) double cream*
2 egg yolks	*2 dessert apples*
juice of ½ lemon	*watercress*

Chop the onion finely, and sweat in the melted butter until tender, but not brown. Add the curry powder, hot stock, and cornflour, slaked in a little cold water. Bring to the boil, stirring. Simmer for 10 minutes. Add egg yolks to the warmed cream. Work a little soup into this mixture, then add it to the soup as a liaison. Mix thoroughly, then remove from the heat. Blend in one of the apples, peeled, cored, and thinly sliced. Season to taste. Chill. Peel, core and finely dice the other apple, and leave to macerate in the lemon juice. Just before serving, add the apple, and decorate each serving with a little chopped watercress.

Cold Curried Cream of Aubergine Soup

560 g (1¼ lb) aubergine
2 onions
60 g (2 oz) butter
2 teaspoons curry powder
1 litre (1¾ pints) chicken stock

210 ml (1½ gills) double
  cream
parsley
salt and white pepper

Trim and peel the aubergine, and cut it into small cubes. Chop the onions, and sauté them gently in the butter. Stir in the curry powder, and cook over moderately low heat, stirring, for 2 minutes. Add the aubergine and the chicken stock, and bring to the boil. Simmer the mixture, covered, for 45 minutes, or until the aubergine is very soft. Purée the mixture in a blender, and strain the purée through a fine sieve into a bowl. Add the cream and salt and pepper to taste. Chill for at least 3 hours. Before serving, sprinkle with chopped parsley.

Avgolemono Soupa (Greek Egg and Lemon Soup)

1¼ litres (2½ pints) vegetable
  stock
3 eggs
juice of 1 or 2 lemons

sea salt, black pepper
2 tablespoons brown rice,
  vermicelli or soya flakes

Bring the stock to the boil, throw in the rice, and simmer for 20 minutes. Beat the eggs until frothy, then add the lemon juice and a tablespoon of cold water. Take a ladleful of hot stock, and add it gradually to the egg and lemon. Add another ladleful, then pour all the liquor back into the stock pan, and stir away from the heat. Add more stock if too thick. Heat very gently, season as necessary, and serve at once. Take care not to boil, or the eggs will curdle.

Iced Avocado Soup

2 ripe avocado pears
2 teaspoons lemon juice
¾ litre (1¼ pints) strong
    chicken stock

3 chopped spring onions, white
    part only
280 ml (½ pint) cream
salt and white pepper
chopped olives or watercress

Peel the avocados, remove stones, and place with the lemon juice in the container of an electric liquidizer. Blend to a smooth purée, and mix with the stock. Add the finely-chopped onions, and heat gently in a bain-marie. When hot, blend in the cream, stirring constantly until the mixture is smooth. Cook over simmering water for 15 minutes, stirring occasionally. Season to taste. Strain, and chill. Serve very cold with a garnish of chopped olives or watercress.

Cold Borshch

2¼ litres (4 pints) strong beef
    stock
900 g (2 lb) uncooked beetroot
2 carrots
1 onion

2 teaspoons white wine
    vinegar
4 tablespoons soured cream
1 tablespoon chopped chives
salt and white pepper

Peel the beetroot and chop into small pieces. Chop the peeled carrots and onion. Simmer the vegetables in the stock until tender and until the soup is a deep red. Strain, and add vinegar and season to taste. Chill, and serve very cold with a tablespoonful of soured cream and a few chopped chives to garnish each serving.

Turkish Cacik

6 cucumbers
1⅛ litres (2 pints) yoghourt
1 teaspoon salt

6 tablespoons sesame oil, or
  substitute olive or corn oil

Peel and thinly slice the cucumbers. Place in a colander with a sprinkling of salt to drain for ½ hour. Dry the cucumber slices, and mix with all the other ingredients. Chill until ice cold.

Cold Carrot Soup

225 g (8 oz) carrots
1 tablespoon grated onion
2 tablespoons peanut butter

280 ml (½ pint) milk
dash of sherry

Clean, scrape and slice the carrots. Boil them gently in just enough water to cover until tender (25–30 minutes). Add the grated onion and the peanut butter. Stir and simmer for a further 10 minutes. Sieve or blend. Add the milk, and mix thoroughly. Add a dash of sherry, and chill thoroughly. A single blue borage flower or a chive blossom may be floated on top of each serving as decorative garnish.

Potage Crème d'Or

1 medium onion, chopped
450 g (1 lb) carrots
45 g (1½ oz) butter
560 ml (1 pint) white stock
1 heaped teaspoon arrowroot

280 ml (½ pint) fresh orange
  juice
210 ml (1½ gills) single cream
nutmeg
chives or parsley

Melt the butter in a heavy pan, add the onion and the carrots (peeled and thinly sliced), and sweat gently for approximately 10 to 20 minutes. Pour in hot stock, and simmer until carrots are very tender. Blend to a purée. Return purée to the cleaned pan. Slake the arrowroot in one dessertspoon cold water, and use to thicken the soup.

Cook it a few minutes, then draw aside and add the orange juice; then the cream. Adjust seasoning, and add a scraping of nutmeg. Serve hot or chilled. Scatter chopped chives or parsley on top, and, if desired, a dab of cream.

Cherry Soup

450 g (1 lb) cherries
scant 280 ml (½ pint) red
  wine
piece of cinnamon bark

piece of lemon peel
1½ teaspoons potato flour
1 dessertspoon sugar
rusks

Stone the cherries, and boil them in 280 ml (½ pint) hot water for 10 minutes, along with the cinnamon bark and the lemon peel. Put the mixture through a sieve. Crush the cherry stones in a mortar, and boil them with the red wine for about 10 minutes gently. Strain through muslin, and add to the cherry purée. Slake the potato flour in a little cold water, and stir into the boiling soup. Season with sugar, and pour very hot into a tureen or into serving bowls. Crumble a few rusks, and sprinkle on top of each serving.

Iced Curried Chicken Soup

1⅛ litres (2 pints) well-
  flavoured chicken stock
½ tablespoon curry powder
140 ml (¼ pint) cream

1 tablespoon chopped parsley
2 teaspoons grated lemon rind
salt and pepper
1 lemon

Dissolve the curry powder in a little of the stock over low heat. Add to the rest of the stock, and cool. Stir in the cream, parsley and lemon rind. Season with salt and pepper. Serve well chilled with a translucent slice of lemon adrift in each cup.

Iced Coconut and Aubergine Soup

1 litre (1¾ pints) stock
225 g (8 oz) freshly grated
   coconut, or 140 g (5 oz)
   dessicated coconut
1 large aubergine, peeled and
   chopped

1 tablespoon chopped parsley
1 teaspoon ground ginger
juice of 1 lemon or lime
2 teaspoons Worcestershire
   sauce
salt and pepper

Bring stock to the boil. Add aubergine, coconut and parsley; ginger, lemon juice and Worcestershire sauce. Season to taste. Simmer for 1½ hours. If too much reduced, add more stock. Chill before serving, and sprinkle with paprika.

Cold Cucumber Soup

2 small cucumbers
1⅛ litres (2 pints) white stock
280 ml (½ pint) soured cream

grated lemon rind
salt and pepper
chives

Peel and dice the cucumbers. Add to the white stock in a heavy saucepan, and cook gently until cucumber is soft. Cool slightly, and mouli or blend along with the soured cream. Season with grated lemon rind to taste, and salt and pepper. Chill thoroughly, and serve very cold with chopped chives sprinkled on top.

Crème de Concombres Glacé

1 cucumber
2 medium onions
a sprig of mint
45 g (1½ oz) butter
1 tablespoonful flour

70 ml (½ gill) cream
¾ litre (1¼ pints) milk and
   water mixed
1 white of egg
salt and pepper

Skin half the cucumber. Cut it into shreds, and put into a pan with the sliced onions. Pour over the milk and water, and add salt and pepper. Simmer gently until vegetables are tender. Sieve or blend the mixture. Melt the butter in a soup pan. Take off the heat, and add the flour, stirring. Pour on the cucumber mixture, and stir over the heat until it comes to the boil. Add the chopped mint and simmer for 6 minutes. Remove and cool. Whip the cream lightly. Add to it the stiffly beaten egg white, and mix into the soup with the remainder of the cucumber, cut into shreds and blanched. Chill, and serve very cold, with a little cream on top if desired.

Cucumber Jelly

2 large peeled cucumbers
½ small onion
½ tablespoon lemon juice
salt and pepper
1 teaspoon finely-chopped mint

280 ml (½ pint) aspic jelly, unset
60 g (2 oz) prawns, previously cooked

Grate the cucumber. Grate the onion, and mix with the cucumber. Season with lemon juice, salt and pepper. Mix with the liquid aspic jelly and the chopped mint. Pour into dishes and leave to set. Garnish with prawns, and serve with hot buttered garlic bread.

Cucumber Vichyssoise

450 g (1 lb) potatoes
1 peeled cucumber
1 onion
15 g (½ oz) butter

560 ml (1 pint) white or vegetable stock
140 ml (¼ pint) cream or top milk

Peel and dice the potatoes. Cut the cucumber into chunks. Chop the onion. Heat the butter in a soup pan, and add the vegetables, turning to coat them with butter. Add the stock, bring to the boil, and simmer until tender, about ½ hour. Sieve or blend, and taste for seasoning. If serving hot, add top of the milk before final heating. If serving cold, add cream and chill thoroughly. A handful of watercress, sorrel or mint leaves sprinkled on top enhances the soup.

Finnish Summer Soup

6 small new potatoes, peeled
   and halved
420 ml (¾ pint) water
2 teaspoons salt
¼ teaspoon white pepper
30 g (1 oz) butter
4 tiny pickling onions, or
   spring onions
16 baby carrots

225 g (8 oz) young French
   beans, cut in 2½ cm (1 in)
   lengths
225 g (8 oz) shelled new
   peas
scant 560 ml (1 pint) half
   milk, half cream
3 tablespoons flour

Cook the potatoes in the simmering water for about 5 minutes. Add salt, pepper, butter, onions, carrots, and green beans, and simmer 8 minutes more. Add the peas, and cook another 2 minutes. All the vegetables should be crisp. Mix together the cream and flour until smooth. Stir into the simmering vegetables, and cook gently for a further 5 minutes, stirring.

Cold Fish Chowder

4 leeks
1 onion
30 g (1 oz) butter
6 potatoes
1⅛ litres (2 pints) white fish
   stock

1⅛ litres (2 pints) milk
450 g (1 lb) flaked cooked
   white fish
280 ml (½ pint) double cream
chives

Wash and slice the leeks, and sauté in the butter with the sliced onion in a covered saucepan until soft. Add the peeled and thinly sliced potatoes, and the stock, which can be made from the skin and bones of the fish. Bring to the boil, and simmer, covered, for about 20 minutes. Add the milk and the fish, bring to the boil, then purée through a food mill or sieve. Cool, stir in the cream, and chill for at least 4 hours. Serve garnished with snipped chives.

Gazpacho

8 large ripe tomatoes
½ Spanish onion
1 small green pepper
1 cucumber
420 ml (¾ pint) tomato juice
30 g (1 oz) butter
4 spring onions

6 tablespoons olive oil
4 tablespoons lemon juice
salt
cayenne
2 slices bread for croûtons
2 garlic cloves, crushed and
    chopped

Skin, seed and chop the tomatoes, reserving two for garnish. Blend 6 tomatoes with the tomato juice, one garlic clove, 1 or 2 tablespoons juice of a finely-grated onion, and ½ cucumber, peeled and cubed. Purée mixture in an electric liquidizer, and chill. Just before serving, blend in olive oil, lemon juice, salt and cayenne. Heat the butter with the other garlic clove, add cubes of bread, and fry until golden. Put very cold Gazpacho on the table, and surround with one dish finely-chopped green pepper, one dish finely-chopped spring onion, one dish finely-chopped tomato, one dish finely-chopped half cucumber, and a dish of croûtons.

Cordoba Gazpacho

2 cloves garlic
2 cucumbers
2 tablespoons olive oil
420 ml (¾ pint) water

420 ml (¾ pint) double cream
2 teaspoons cornflour
1 teaspoon salt

Mix thoroughly the crushed cloves of garlic, the peeled, seeded and cubed cucumbers, and the olive oil. Bring the water to the boil with the salt. Slake the cornflour in 3 tablespoons water, and add to the boiling water. Stir the mixture, and when the water has thickened and you can no longer taste the cornflour, pour the mixture over the garlic, cucumbers and oil. Let it cool, and add the cream very gradually. Chill, and serve very cold.

Iced Haddock Soup

110 g (4 oz) smoked haddock   *1 tablespoon chives*
560 ml (1 pint) milk   *½ tablespoon grated onion*
280 ml (½ pint) yoghourt   *lemon juice*
1 peeled cucumber   *black pepper*
2 tablespoons chopped parsley   *red caviar*

Poach the haddock in the milk. Cook, strain off and reserve the milk, and flake the haddock. Add the yoghourt to the milk and mix well. Add the haddock, chopped cucumber, parsley, chives and onion. Season well with freshly-ground black pepper and a little lemon juice. Serve well-chilled with a garnish of red caviar.

Greek Tarata

3 green peppers   *½ teaspoon pepper*
6 aubergines   *pinch of cayenne*
6 tablespoons olive oil   *pinch of powdered mint*
1 litre (1¾ pints) yoghourt   *2 crushed cloves of garlic*
1 teaspoon salt

Skin and seed the peppers, and skin and salt the aubergines. Leave aubergines cut side down on a tea towel to sweat for 30 minutes. Wipe dry, and squeeze gently to remove all bitter juices. Sauté the peppers and aubergines in the oil until tender, but do not brown. Purée in a blender, then mix thoroughly with the yoghourt. Add salt, pepper, cayenne, mint and garlic. Serve ice cold.

Iced Lemon Soup

4 egg yolks   *560 ml (1 pint) white stock*
juice of 2 lemons   *140 ml (¼ pint) cream*
grated rind of ½ lemon   *chopped chives*
140 ml (¼ pint) soured cream

Beat the yolks with the lemon rind. Blend in the lemon juice and the soured cream. Heat the stock, and gradually add to the yolks, stirring continually. Cook over a very low flame or in the top of a bain-marie over simmering water, stirring until the mixture thickens, as you would for a custard. Remove from heat, and add the cream, then season with salt and pepper. Cool, stirring occasionally. Serve well chilled in cups, garnished with chopped chives. Hot cheese straws make a nice accompaniment.

Lettuce and Cucumber Soup

1 small lettuce
1 large onion, sliced
2 rashers bacon or ham
　trimmings, chopped
60 g (2 oz) butter
110 g (4 oz) shelled peas
2 dessertspoons flour
280 ml (½ pint) milk

1 tablespoon chopped fresh
　mint, and a pinch of dried
　mixed herbs
280 ml (½ pint) stock or
　bouillon
1 peeled cucumber
salt and lemon juice
mint and croûtons, or paprika
　and double cream to garnish

Wash and shred the lettuce. Fry onion and bacon gently in butter until transparent. Add the shredded lettuce and peas. Cover and cook over low heat for 10 minutes, shaking the pan. Turn off the heat, and stir in sufficient flour to absorb the fat. Mix in milk, and bring to the boil. Add herbs and thin as required with stock. Grate half the cucumber, and stir into the soup with salt to taste. Cover and simmer gently for about 30 minutes, or until peas are tender. Sieve or purée in a blender, and adjust the seasoning with salt and lemon juice.

To serve hot, sprinkle with fresh chopped mint, and hand round a bowl of fried croûtons. To serve cold, after puréeing the mixture, grate in the remaining half cucumber (peeled), keeping 4 thin slices for garnish. Season well with salt and lemon juice, and chill throughly. Serve with a dab of cream and a thin slice of cucumber sprinkled with paprika.

Iced Cream of Mushroom Soup

840 ml (1½ pints) strong
  chicken stock
225 g (8 oz) mushrooms
1 tablespoon arrowroot

280 ml (½ pint) creamy milk
140 ml (¼ pint) single cream
snipped chives

Bring the stock to the boil in a soup pan. Add the washed and sliced mushrooms, and simmer for 10 minutes. Blend the mixture, or force it through a sieve. Return to the clean pan, and simmer for 5 to 10 minutes. Mix arrowroot with cold milk, add, and bring to the boil. Season to taste. Chill. Just before serving, whisk cream to a froth and add to the soup. Serve with a sprinkling of chives.

Pawpaw Soup

30 g (1 oz) butter
1 finely-chopped onion
1 large unripe pawpaw, peeled
  and cut into pieces
560 ml (1 pint) stock

salt and pepper
1 tablespoon finely-chopped
  parsley
140 ml (¼ pint) milk

Fry onion and pawpaw in butter, but do not brown. Add stock, salt and pepper to taste, and simmer until pawpaw is soft. Rub through a sieve, add milk, re-heat and add sufficient beurre manié to give the desired thickness. Serve sprinkled with parsley.

Polish Chlodnik

60 g (2 oz) lean veal
60 g (2 oz) raw beetroot
1 teaspoon chives
1 teaspoon powdered dill
225 g (8 oz) prawns

1 teaspoon salt
½ teaspoon pepper
1 cucumber
420 ml (¾ pint) soured cream
6 hard-boiled eggs

Cut the veal into small pieces and simmer for 20 minutes in water to cover, skimming. Cook the beetroot until tender, and sieve it, retaining the water in which it was cooked.

Peel the cucumber, and slice it very thinly. Add the cucumber to the beetroot and its water. Add the veal and gradually stir in the soured cream, then add the dill, salt and pepper, chives cut into small bits, the prawns, and last, the sliced hard-boiled eggs. Chill, and serve very cold.

Potage Germiny (Sorrel Soup)

450 g (1 lb) sorrel	*3 egg yolks*
30 g (1 oz) butter	*140 ml (¼ pint) cream*
1¼ litres (2½ pints) white	*salt and pepper*
stock	*chervil*

Wash and shred the sorrel. Soften it in the melted butter. Add the stock, and simmer for 15 minutes. Sieve or blend, and return to the clean pan. Thicken with a liaison of the yolks diluted with the cream. Heat and stir until slightly thickened, but on no account allow it to boil, as the acid in the sorrel will curdle the mixture. Taste for seasoning. Chill, and serve very cold with a sprinkling of chervil for each serving.

Chilled Spinach Soup

450 g (1 lb) fresh spinach, or	*3 spring onions*
400 g (14 oz) packet	*1½ tablespoons lemon juice*
frozen	*salt and pepper*
140 ml (¼ pint) soured cream	*white stock*
1 small cucumber	

Wash the spinach thoroughly if fresh, let defrost if frozen. Place it in a covered saucepan, and cook until just tender – about 6 minutes. Drain it, reserving the liquid. Put it through the mouli or blender, and add the spinach water augmented by enough stock to make up to ¾ litre (1½ pints) liquid. Bring this mixture to the boiling point. Remove it from the heat, and add the lemon juice. Chill thoroughly. When quite cold, stir the spinach mixture into the soured cream, and add the diced cucumber (which you have first sprinkled with salt and drained for ½ hour), and the minced spring onions. Season with salt and freshly-ground black pepper. Chill again.

Summer Soup

1 lettuce	*1 chicken stock cube*
1 bunch watercress	*420 ml (¾ pint) milk*
6 spring onions	*salt*
45 g (1½ oz) butter	*black pepper*
420 ml (¾ pint) water	*140 ml (¼ pint) double cream*

Shred lettuce and watercress, including watercress stalks. Roughly chop spring onions, including tops. Melt butter in soup pan, add lettuce, watercress and onion, and soften over gentle heat with the lid on the pan. Add the water, which has been turned into stock with the cube. Add the milk, and season to taste with pepper and salt. Bring all to the boil, and simmer gently for 15 minutes. Sieve or blend, and return to the washed pan. Heat through, and when ready to serve, add half the cream and mix into the soup. Reserve remainder of cream, and spoon a bit on top of each serving.

Iced Tomato Cream

1 onion	*70 ml (½ gill) soured cream*
15 g (½ oz) butter	*½ teaspoon tomato paste*
6 tomatoes	*½ teaspoon sugar*
140 ml (¼ pint) chicken stock	*½ teaspoon thyme*
210 ml (1½ gills) double cream	*½ teaspoon salt*
	1 lime or lemon

Chop the onion and sweat in the butter in a covered saucepan until soft. Add the peeled, seeded, and chopped tomatoes, the chicken stock and the tomato paste, sugar, thyme and salt. Simmer the mixture, covered, for 10 minutes. Cool, and purée in a blender with the two creams, and lime or lemon juice, salt and pepper to taste. Sieve, and chill in the freezing compartment of the refrigerator for 1 hour. Garnish each serving with a thin slice of lime or lemon and a sprig of parsley.

Vichyssoise

3 medium leeks
1 medium onion
4 medium potatoes
salt and pepper
small bunch watercress

60 g (2 oz) butter
140 ml (¼ pint) cream
1⅛ litres (2 pints) chicken
   stock

Sweat the cleaned and sliced white part of the leeks along with the sliced onion in the butter. Do not allow it to brown. Add the peeled and sliced potatoes and the stock. Season and simmer until tender. Sieve or blend. Cool a little, and stir in the cream and the finely-chopped watercress. Serve either well chilled, or hot with grated cheese sprinkled on top.

Note: Vichyssoise is included here more as a *chilled* than a summer soup, as leeks are primarily a winter vegetable.

Chinese Watercress Soup

1 litre (1¾ pints) chicken stock
3 tablespoons shredded
   cooked pork
60 g (2 oz) finely-sliced celery,
   cut on the diagonal

60 g (2 oz) sliced water
   chestnuts or bamboo shoots
2 sliced spring onions
1 tablespoon soya sauce
leaves from 1 bunch watercress

Combine chicken stock, pork, celery, water chestnuts or bamboo shoots, spring onions and soya sauce. Bring to the boil, and simmer for 5 minutes. Add watercress, and serve very hot.

Yoghourt Soup

2 large cucumbers   salt and pepper
560 ml (1 pint) yoghourt   1 clove garlic
2 tablespoons chopped walnuts

Peel the cucumbers and cut into very thin slices. Sprinkle with 2 teaspoons salt, and leave in a cool place for ½ hour. Put into a large bowl the yoghourt, crushed garlic and salt and pepper to taste, and mix well. Drain the liquid from the cucumber slices, dry them, and add them to the yoghourt mixture. Serve very cold with a sprinkling of chopped walnuts on each serving.

Iced Yoghourt and Prawn Soup

560 ml (1 pint) yoghourt   1 tablespoon chopped chives
280 ml (½ pint) cream   salt and pepper
110 g (4 oz) prawns   chopped mint, or paprika
1 medium cucumber

Combine the yoghourt and cream, and mix well. Peel and grate the cucumber. Mix it into the yoghourt with the prawns and chives. Season with salt and pepper. Serve well-chilled with a garnish of chopped mint, or with a little paprika sprinkled on top.

CHAPTER NINE

Time-Saving Soups

WHILE THIS BOOK MAKES NO attempt to debase the art
of soup-making by suggesting that you mix a tin of tomato
soup with one of green pea to produce a simplified 'purée
mongole', I have included a selection of soups which can be
quickly and easily made, and which are delicious and
wholesome as well. Some of these soups can only be made
quickly if you have fresh or frozen (see p. 17) home-made
stock on hand, notably those based on fish stock, for which
there is no short cut. Others can be satisfactorily made by
the addition of a stock cube.

The temptation to concoct a quick soup out of a casual
conglomeration of left-overs should be resisted. Old mashed
potatoes when combined with Sunday's chicken carcass
and a few bruised vegetable leaves will not produce a quick
vichyssoise, nor will an overdose of chili powder conceal the
flavour extracted from stale fish. Ingredients, whether fresh
or left-over, should never be randomly combined for the

sake of speed. Some flavours simply refuse to mix, even with
the aid of a liquidizer. Beware of recipes that instruct you,
for example, to make 'green chili soup' by combining the
contents of a tin of green chilies with 3 tablespoons of
chunky peanut butter, 1 tablespoon tomato ketchup, and
3 cups of tinned chicken broth. This combination is said to
give an Indonesian character to the soup. I do not recommend it.

I *do* recommend the following soups as simple to make
and satisfying to eat. They can all be made in half an hour
or less, and the first on the list can be made in 15 minutes,
provided that all the materials are at hand. It is called:

Sopa de Cuarto de Hore (Quarter-of-an-Hour Soup)

1¼ litres (2 pints) well-
seasoned fish stock
225 g (8 oz) long grain rice
handful of peeled shrimps

handful of chopped ham
2 hard-boiled eggs
chopped parsley

Bring fish stock to the boil. Add the rice, the shrimps, the
roughly chopped hard-boiled eggs, and the ham. Simmer all
together until the rice is cooked, about fifteen minutes. A
glass of very dry sherry may be added at the last moment.
Sprinkle chopped parsley on top, and serve very hot.

Angel's Soup

1½ litres (2½ pints) chicken
broth
1 small tin asparagus tips
(298 g/10½ oz)
110 g (4 oz) button mushrooms

4 small hard-boiled eggs,
chopped
pinch monosodium glutamate
(optional)
salt and pepper

Bring the broth to the boil. Add all the other ingredients and
seasonings. Cover and simmer very gently for 8–10 minutes.
Serve very hot.

Avocado Soup

2 large ripe avocados
140 ml (¼ pint) cream
1 tablespoon butter
1 tablespoon flour

1 finely-chopped onion
1 litre (1¾ pints) stock
salt and pepper
croûtons

Fry onion in butter, add flour, mixing well, then gradually add stock. Season with salt and pepper, simmer until smooth. Combine with mashed avocados and cream. Beat thoroughly, and heat but do not boil. Serve with croûtons.

Beer Soup

45 g (1½ oz) butter
4 tablespoons flour
1¾ litres (3 pints) light beer
salt and pepper

cinnamon
sugar
140 ml (1¼ pint) double
cream

Make a roux of the butter and flour. Stir in the beer slowly. Season with salt, pepper and cinnamon, and add a teaspoon of sugar. Boil for several minutes. Bind with the cream and pour very hot over slices of toast.

Beggarman's Soup

4 slices rye bread
4 eggs
butter

1⅛ litres (2 pints) good stock
chopped parsley

Toast the bread lightly and butter well. Cut into cubes and place in 4 oven-proof soup bowls. Bring the stock to the boil, and as it boils, break an egg onto the toast in each plate and sprinkle with parsley. Pour the stock over, and place the bowls over a very low heat for several minutes, until the eggs are lightly poached.

Gill's Cabbage Soup

110 g (4 oz) fat bacon
30 g (1 oz) oil or butter
½ small cabbage

1 tablespoonful flour
280 ml (½ pint) beef stock
280–560 ml (½–1 pint) milk

Cut the bacon into strips, and fry in the fat until just lightly browned; not crisp. Shred the cabbage, and stir-fry with the bacon for about 5 minutes. Add the flour, and gradually stir in the beef stock and 280 ml (½ pint) milk. Simmer for 15 minutes, diluting with additional milk if desired.

Cheese Soup

1¼ litres (2½ pints) water
280 ml (½ pint) soured cream
3 large potatoes
chopped parsley

85 g (3 oz) grated Parmesan
   cheese
salt
30 g (1 oz) butter

Peel potatoes and cook in salted water. Blend in an electric liquidizer, return to the clean pan, and add grated cheese. Simmer for a few minutes, then add cream and butter. Tip from side to side to blend, and just before serving, add chopped parsley.

Swiss Chestnut Soup

1 medium tin unsweetened
   chestnut purée (440 g/15½ oz)
1 litre (1¾ pints) vegetable
   stock
1 teaspoon celery salt
1 teaspoon brown sugar

grated rind of a lemon
420 ml (¾ pint) milk
2 tablespoons brown flour
2 knobs butter
yoghourt or soured cream
pepper

Mix the purée with the stock, celery salt, sugar and lemon rind, add the milk, and simmer for 15 minutes. Add the flour, mixed to a smooth paste with cold water. Heat to boiling point, then stir in the butter. Serve with a dab of yoghourt or soured cream on top of each serving.

Scrap Chicken Soup

1 litre (1¾ pints) good chicken
stock, trimmings and scraps
from a chicken carcass

Put half the stock in the liquidizer with the chicken trimmings, and blend until smooth. Gradually add the rest of the stock. Season. Serve very hot.

Cucumber Soup

450 g (1 lb) chopped cucumber   *generous ¾ litre (1¼ pints)*
1 chopped onion   *white stock*
45 g (1½ oz) butter   *280 ml (½ pint) cream*
1 teaspoon chopped parsley   *60 g (2 oz) flour*
                                      salt and white pepper

Toss the cucumber, onion, and parsley in the butter over low heat until tender. Do not brown. Add the flour, stirring. Remove from heat, cool slightly, and add the cream. Add the hot stock gradually. Season to taste, and serve very hot.

Egg Drop Soup

4 chicken cubes   *225 g (8 oz) peeled, seeded,*
1 litre (1¾ pints) hot water   *diced tomato*
                                      1 egg

Dissolve chicken cubes in hot water, add tomato, and simmer for 5 minutes. Beat the egg, and add it to the soup, stirring constantly for a minute or two until it separates into threads. Serve at once.

Mushroom Soup

3 0 g *(12 oz) mushrooms*
6 g *(2 oz) butter*
garlic
parsley
nutmeg

1 thick slice of bread
1 litre (1¾ pints) white stock
scant 140 ml (¼ pint) cream
salt and pepper

Clean the mushrooms, and cut them in small pieces. Melt the butter in a heavy pan, add the mushrooms, and sweat gently until their moisture starts to run. Add a small piece of chopped garlic, a tablespoon of chopped parsley, a seasoning of salt and freshly-ground black pepper, and grated nutmeg. Simmer together for 2 minutes. Soak the bread in a little stock, squeeze out the moisture, and add to the mushroom mixture. Stir until blended, add the stock, and simmer for 15 minutes. Blend the soup in an electric liquidizer. Return to the clean pan, re-heat, and add the boiling cream and a tablespoon of finely-chopped parsley.

Creamy Mushroom Soup

140 ml (¼ pint) soured cream
560 ml (1 pint) water
4 large potatoes
60 g (2 oz) flour
225 g (8 oz) fresh mushrooms

1 tablespoon dill weed
1 egg
few caraway seeds
vinegar
salt

Clean and cut up the mushrooms. Simmer in the water with caraway seeds for about 10 minutes. Mix the cream into the flour, and gradually add the mushroom mixture. Add diced raw potatoes. Cook for about 15 minutes. Pour a little of this mixture into the well-beaten egg, and mix into the soup. Add salt to taste, a few drops of vinegar, and the chopped dill. Heat, but do not boil.

My Soup

1 tablespoon chopped onion
*1 tablespoon chopped green
    pepper*
30 g (1 oz) butter
30 g (1 oz) flour
*1 small tin tomatoes
    (225 g/8 oz)*
840 ml (1½ pints) brown stock

*1 small packet frozen spinach
    (225 g/8 oz)*
*1 small packet frozen petits
    pois (225 g/8 oz)*
1 dessertspoon lemon juice
*1 tablespoon grated horse-
    radish*
3 tablespoons whipped cream

Sweat the onion and the green pepper in the melted butter.
Sprinkle with the flour, and stir until blended. Stir in the
tomatoes, the spinach and the peas. Pour on the beef stock,
and bring to the boil. Simmer for about 5 minutes, until
peas are tender. Sieve or blend. Return to a clean pan. Add
the lemon juice, the horseradish, and finish with the whipped
cream.

Rosie's Quick French Onion Soup

*340 g (12 oz) frozen chopped
    onion*
*1¾ litres (3 pints) strong beef
    stock*

15 g (½ oz) butter
sugar
French bread
Parmesan cheese

Fry the onions in the butter until very brown. Sprinkle on a
little sugar to caramelize. Pour on the hot stock, stirring
well. Toast slices of French bread, and float on top of the
soup just before serving. Sprinkle lavishly with Parmesan
cheese.

Purée Saint-Germain Simple

1 kg (2¼ lb) fresh peas
1⅛ litres (2 pints) white stock

60 g (2 oz) butter
chervil

Shell the peas, and cook quickly in salted water until tender,
but not mushy. Rub all but 2 tablespoons of the peas through
a sieve, reserving the rest. Put the purée back into the clean

pan, and add the white stock. Bring to the boil, swirl in the butter, add the reserved whole peas, and garnish with a sprinkling of chervil leaves.

Spinach Soup

1 kg (2¼ lb) spinach or 1 large packet, chopped, frozen	*280 ml (½ pint) stock*
	280 ml (½ pint) milk
1 tablespoon grated onion	*salt*
30 g (1 oz) butter	*grated nutmeg*
30 g (1 oz) flour	*2 tablespoons grated cheese*

Thoroughly wash spinach, if fresh. If frozen, melt in a saucepan with a nut of butter, and set aside. Cook fresh spinach in a little boiling water until tender; 5 minutes should be enough for this. Drain, and sieve or purée in a blender. Melt the butter in a saucepan. Add onion, and cook over medium heat until transparent. Add flour, and stir until blended. Gradually add stock and milk, stirring until smooth. Add puréed (or frozen, cooked) spinach, and season with salt and a little grated nutmeg. Add more stock if the soup is too thick. Serve hot with grated cheese sprinkled on top.

Quick Cream of Tomato Soup

¾ litre (1¼ pints) milk	*pinch sugar*
225 g (8 oz) chopped fresh tomatoes, or 1 medium tin (396 g/14 oz)	*salt and pepper*
	croûtons

Combine cold milk and tomatoes. Heat slowly until simmering; not boiling. Season to taste, sieve, and serve hot with croûtons.

Tortellini in Brodo

A very good dried Italian tortellini can now be bought in speciality food shops and turned into this quick and excellent soup.

110 g (4 oz) dried Italian tortellini

1¼ litres (2½ pints) strong beef stock
Parmesan cheese

Cook the tortellini according to the instructions on the packet. Make beef stock from 2 or 3 stock cubes. Pour the stock into soup bowls, and float the tortellini in the soup. Serve with Parmesan cheese.

Tyrolean Soup with Pancakes

1⅛ litres (2 pints) good veal or beef stock

4 thin pancakes
salt and pepper

Heat the stock. Shred the pancakes. Drop them into the stock, and simmer for several minutes before serving.

Walnut Soup

170 g (6 oz) shelled walnuts
up to 1⅛ litres (2 pints) white stock
large clove garlic

140 ml (¼ pint) cream
salt
freshly-ground black pepper

Crush walnuts and garlic to a paste with a little stock, using a liquidizer or pestle and mortar. Incorporate the rest of the stock slowly until the mixture is the consistency of single cream. If the walnuts have been liquidized, they will take up most of the stock; if pounded, somewhat less. Put the soup through a sieve into a saucepan, and bring the mixture to the boil. Add cream, and correct the seasoning with salt and pepper.

CHAPTER TEN

Consommés

A CONSOMME IS SIMPLY A clear soup with the addition of various light garnishes. Although somewhat out of favour today, consommé remains a fine start to a rich meal, for reasons perhaps best expressed by Prosper Montagné, 'Clear soup is a food of mediocre nutritive value, but an excellent 'quickener' of digestion and a stimulant which tones up the heart and slightly raises the blood pressure. It has an action, so far still shrouded in mystery, similar to that of coffee and chocolate, which, from the moment it is ingested, creates the sensation of well-being, before a small part of it can be absorbed.'

Consommés have been named for princesses, chefs, admirals, musicians; and they range from the relatively simple to the vastly elaborate. Simple consommés, properly made, are fine on their own. Clever cooks will contrive suitable accompaniments. Elaborate consommés are really not the province of the home cook, but recipes for them are included in this section to provide glimpses of past eating habits. Mock Turtle Soup is not much seen these days, but Eliza Acton devoted two entire pages of her *Modern Cookery* to its construction. A shorter version appears here. Green

Turtle Soup is a relic of halcyon country house days, when
sea turtles were more abundantly imported, and oysters
were food for the poor. It is included as a rarity.

Materials for inclusion in the stock pot should be carefully chosen. Used sensibly, a stock pot is an economy, and
provides a valuable base for soups and sauces of all sorts; it
should never be used as a culinary compost heap. For basic
stock recipes, see Some Notes on Stock, p. 15.

To Clarify Consommé

To clarify consommé or any meat or vegetable stock, first
let the liquid get quite cold. Then remove every speck of
fat and measure the stock or consommé. For every 1⅛ litres
(2 pints) stock, you need 1 egg white and 1 eggshell. Beat
the egg white slightly and add to it 2 teaspoons cold water.
Add this to the stock with the fractured eggshell. Stir over
a low flame until the mixture boils. Boil it for 2 minutes.
Remove from the fire and leave for 20 minutes. Strain it
through a fine sieve placed over a larger fine sieve which is
lined with a double thickness of muslin.
Note: in recipes in which the consommé has to be thickened
with arrowroot, starch or tapioca, the liaison should be
light; just enough to mellow the consommé slightly. As a
guide, use a maximum of 3 tablespoons tapioca per 1⅛
litres (2 pints) of liquid; 2 tablespoons of arrowroot or cornflour per 1⅛ litres (2 pints) of liquid. All garnished consommés thickened with arrowroot or tapioca should be
strained through muslin as soon as the liaison is complete.

Consommé à l'Alsacienne

To 1⅛ litres (2 pints) brown stock, add 225 g (8 oz) sauerkraut cooked in stock, and a Strasbourg sausage, which has
been poached, skinned and cut into rounds.

Consommé à l'Ambassadrice

Lightly thicken 1⅛ litres (2 pints) chicken stock with tapioca. Strain, garnish with 24 small truffled chicken quenelles and 12 small profiteroles filled with purée of foie gras and chervil leaves.

Consommé à l'Amiral

Thicken 1⅛ litres (2 pints) fish stock with arrowroot. Strain and garnish with 24 small whiting or pike forcemeat quenelles flavoured with crayfish butter, 6 poached oysters cut in half and de-bearded, and 2 tablespoons julienne of truffles cooked in Madeira. Sprinkle with chervil leaves.

Consommé à la Basquaise

To 1⅛ litres (2 pints) white stock, add 2 tablespoons julienne of sweet peppers cooked in stock, 2 tablespoons of diced tomatoes cooked in stock, and 4 tablespoons of rice cooked in stock. Sprinkle with chervil leaves.

Consommé Bizet

Thicken 1⅛ litres (2 pints) chicken stock with tapioca. Strain and garnish with tiny chicken quenelles mixed with chopped tarragon leaves. Sprinkle with chervil.

Consommé Brillat-Savarin

Thicken 1⅛ litres (2 pints) chicken stock with tapioca, strain, and garnish with 2 tablespoons of julienne of breast of chicken, 2 tablespoons of savoury pancakes cut into lozenges, 2 tablespoons chiffonnade of lettuce and sorrel and chervil leaves.

Consommé Chasseur

Thicken 1⅛ litres (2 pints) game stock with tapioca. Strain. Garnish with 2 tablespoons of julienne of mushrooms which have been cooked in 70 ml (½ gill) Madeira. Sprinkle with chervil, and serve with 20 small profiteroles filled with game purée.

Consommé à la Florentine

Garnish 1⅛ litres (2 pints) chicken stock with oeufs filés (beaten egg, strained into the hot consommé through a fine strainer, to look like threads). Add 2 tablespoons rice cooked in stock, and chervil leaves.

Consommé Hudson

Colour 1⅛ litres (2 pints) fish stock with tomato juice. Thicken with arrowroot and strain through muslin. Garnish with shredded crab flesh, diced cucumbers cooked in stock, and chervil leaves.

Consommé Nesselrode

Garnish 1⅛ litres (2 pints) game stock with about 30 small profiteroles filled with a mixture of onion and chestnut purée, and very finely chopped mushrooms.

Consommé Nimrod

Thicken 1⅛ litres (2 pints) game stock with arrowroot, and strain. Garnish with tiny quenelles of game forcemeat mixed with chopped truffles, and flavour with 2 tablespoons port.

Consommé with Poached Eggs

Garnish 1⅛ litres (2 pints) white stock with six small poached eggs.

Consommé Princess Alice

Thicken 1⅛ litres (2 pints) chicken stock with tapioca. Strain. Garnish with 1 tablespoon of julienne of artichoke hearts, 1 tablespoon of chiffonade of lettuce, 2 tablespoons fine vermicelli cooked in stock, and chervil leaves.

Cold Consommés

These consommés are usually served as a first course for a summer luncheon or a light supper on a warm evening. I would not choose to serve them at all, having worked through more than my share of unspeakable jellied consommés as a child. But, there are those who like them, so I include a handful of recipes. They must be strongly flavoured and crystal clear.

Consommé Riche

Ingredients for just over 1⅛ litres (2 pints) consommé:

340 g (12 oz) lean beef   *1¾ litres (3 pints) brown stock*
1 carrot   *1 egg white*
1 leek

Remove sinews and gristle from meat and chop it. Chop carrot and slice the white part of the leek. Put the meat, vegetables and egg white into a saucepan with the stock. Bring to the boil, stirring. Simmer very slowly at the side of the stove for 1½ hours. Remove fat and strain through muslin. Chill and serve very cold.

Celery-Flavoured Consommé

Prepare consommé riche. Half an hour before the end of the simmering time, add half a bunch of finely-chopped celery. Finish the cooking, strain through muslin, and chill thoroughly before serving.

Tarragon-Flavoured Consommé

Prepare consommé riche. When the simmering period is over, draw the pan off the fire, and add 4 tablespoons of fresh tarragon leaves. Leave to infuse for 6 minutes, then strain through muslin and chill.

Consommé à la Madrilene

Prepare chicken stock. To 1⅛ litres (2 pints) of this, add 200 g (7 oz) raw tomato pulp which has been put through a sieve. Clarify the consommé, strain through muslin, and chill thoroughly.

TURTLE AND MOCK TURTLE SOUP

Green Turtle Soup

This soup is prepared using the bony carapace and plastron only of a large sea turtle. The outside shields are removed. Cut the carapace and plastron into chunks of equal size, blanch them in boiling water, and put in a big soup pan with a quantity of rich consommé and a few savoury vegetables and herbs. Simmer with the top on the pan for about 5 hours, skimming as necessary. Strain off the stock, and reserve it. Bone the turtle chunks, and cut them into uniform pieces 2½ cm (1 in) square. Keep warm in a bit of strained broth. Strain the stock through several thicknesses of muslin, heat and add 280 ml (½ pint) Madeira or sherry to each 1⅛ litres (2 pints) liquid. Just before serving, put the small pieces of turtle meat back into the soup.

Mock Turtle Soup

Soak a calf's head in water, bone it and cook in white stock flavoured and seasoned with carrots, onion, celery, a bouquet garni, cloves, salt and pepper. When it is cooked, after about 30 minutes' simmering or more depending on its size, drain it, reserving the broth. Cut off the ears, trim the meat, and press it between two plates. When it is cold, cut it into 2½ cm (1 in) square pieces, and keep them hot in a little of the stock. Strain the stock through muslin, and thicken it with a little arrowroot diluted with cold stock. Infuse some basil, spring onions, marjoram, thyme and bay leaf in

Madeira or port, and strain this infusion into the stock mixture. Strain again through muslin, and pour into a soup tureen, after heating it. Garnish with the little pieces of calf's head, and, if liked, small quenelles of forcemeat mixed with pounded hard-boiled yolks of egg.

CHAPTER ELEVEN

Garnishes for Soup

Pasta

Approximately 110 g (4 oz) of vermicelli or any desired pasta should be used for each 1⅛ litres (2 pints) of soup. Cooking time varies from 8 to 14 minutes, depending on the pasta. It may either be added to the soup towards the end of its cooking time, or cooked separately, drained and added to the finished soup.

Rice

Use about 3 tablespoons rice for each 1⅛ litres (2 pints) of soup. Patna rice should be used. Pour boiling water over the rice, then add it to the soup 25 minutes before the end of cooking time. Or, cook the rice in boiling water in a covered pan with salt, drain, and add.

Tapioca or Sago

Use about 110 g (4 oz) per 1⅛ litres (2 pints) of soup. This should be cooked with the soup for 20 minutes.

Printanier

Carrots and turnips cut in fine strips about 2½ cm (1 in) long, diced, or cut out with a small vegetable scoop. Blanch them, then boil them in clear stock. When almost cooked, you may add peas and 2½ cm (1 in) lengths of French beans which have been previously blanched and drained. Blanched asparagus tips may be added at the end as well, if your asparagus bed is over-producing.

Quenelles

These are little balls of poultry, game or fish forcemeat, depending on the construction of the soup to be garnished. They should be not more than 1 cm (½ in) in diameter, which can be accomplished by forcing them through a piping bag with a very small tube. Allow from 5 to 8 tiny quenelles for each serving of soup. The following recipes should be adequate for from 4 to 6 people. Quenelles can be made from raw chicken, pigeon, duck, pheasant, or a soft fish, such as whiting or pike.

Poultry Quenelles

225 (8 oz) trimmed tender
raw poultry flesh
1 egg white

up to 280 ml (½ pint) double
cream
salt and pepper

Cut the flesh into small pieces, having trimmed off any fat, skin and bone. Put the egg white into a blender with a bit of the diced flesh and blend until smooth. Add the rest of the flesh gradually, stopping the motor now and then to stir down the mixture. When it is perfectly smooth, chill it thoroughly, then blend in the cream, little by little. You may not need all the cream. When you think the right consistency is obtained, drop a teaspoonful of the mixture into simmering water, and try. When all is smooth and silky, put the mixture into a forcing bag and pipe into a buttered pan large enough to hold all comfortably. Ten minutes before the soup is to be served, pour boiling salted water over them and simmer slowly. After ten minutes, take up with a slotted spoon, and float them carefully on top of each serving of soup.

Fish Quenelles

2 small egg yolks, or 1 large one
52 g (1¾ oz) flour
30 g (1 oz) melted butter
70 ml (½ gill) hot milk
1 egg white
110 g (4 oz) fat from beef kidney

110 g (4 oz) pike, perch or whiting, without bones or skin
¼ teaspoon salt
pinch pepper
pinch nutmeg

Place the egg yolk in the electric liquidizer with the flour and the melted butter. Blend for 1 minute, and while liquidizer is running, add hot milk and blend all until perfectly smooth. Place this mixture, which is the *panada*, in a small saucepan and cook for about 6 minutes over medium heat, stirring constantly. Put aside to cool. Place in the liquidizer the egg white, the beef kidney fat, which has had all skin removed, and which has been cut into small cubes. When perfectly smooth, remove with a rubber spatula and reserve. Place the cubed fish in the liquidizer with the salt, pepper and nutmeg, and blend at low speed for about 2 minutes. Add the *panada* and the egg white and fat purée. Blend at first at low speed, then high, until very smooth. Pinch off small lozenges of this, and roll them between floured fingers. Poach them for 5 minutes in salted water, taking care that they do not stick to the bottom of the pan, or to each other. Remove from the water with a slotted spoon, and dry on absorbent paper. When you are nearly ready to serve the soup, put the quenelles in to simmer with it for 10 minutes before serving.

Note: these quenelles recipes may be doubled and the quenelles shaped in finger lengths. They then become Godiveau Lyonnaise, and are served as a garnish for

creamed fish, braised chicken or roast veal. Or, they may
be used as an entrée, in which case the final 10 minutes'
simmering will be done in whatever delicate sauce you fancy.

Profiteroles

140 g (5 oz) flour   *3 eggs*
60 g (2 oz) butter   *salt*
280 ml (½ pint) water

Place the water and butter in a saucepan over medium
heat. Stir with a wooden spoon. Sieve the flour onto a piece
of greaseproof paper. When the butter has melted, shoot
the flour into the saucepan all at once. Take the pan off the
heat, and beat hard until the mixture leaves the sides of the
pan. Beat in the eggs one by one, taking care that each one
is thoroughly incorporated in the dough before the next
one is added. Put this mixture into a forcing bag with a
½ cm (¼ in) tube, and pipe little balls the size of a hazelnut
onto a buttered baking sheet. Paint with beaten egg, and
bake in a medium oven (375°, Regulo 5), about 25 minutes.
When they are quite dry, take them out and stuff them with
a purée appropriate to the soup: chicken, foie gras with
cream, or vegetable purée, or a game purée with a chestnut
soup. The little profiteroles may be made ahead of time
and kept in a tin. They should not be stuffed too far in ad-
vance of serving, or they will be soggy instead of crisp.
Allow 4 per head, and serve them in a separate dish to
accompany the soup.

Crêpes for Soup

110 g (4 oz) flour   *2 eggs*
1 teaspoon salt   *350 ml (about ⅔ pint) milk*

Place in a mixing bowl the sieved flour and 1 teaspoon salt.
Add two eggs and mix well. Add the milk, which has been
scalded and cooled slightly. Let this mixture rest for an

hour or so before making the crêpes. Use them as indicated in the soup recipe, or shred them and serve separately as a garnish.

Croûtes à l'Ancienne

1 loaf French bread
butter or fat skimmed from
  pot-au-feu

vegetables from pot-au-feu
grated cheese

Cut the bread into slices 3¼ cm (1½ in) thick. Scoop out ¾ of the bread to make nests. Brush with butter or fat and toast lightly in the oven. Chop or sieve the vegetables, and put a little mound of the mixture into each nest. Sprinkle with grated cheese and moisten with a drop of fat. Brown at the last minute, and serve on a separate dish with a clear soup. This is particularly appropriate for the pot-au-feu broth, as all the ingredients are in the dish except the cheese and bread.

Croûtons

thin slices of stale bread   *butter or oil*

Cut the bread into neat dice (or heart shapes or diamonds), and fry in unsalted butter or oil until golden brown.

Garlic Bread

Slash a stick of French bread with a sharp knife at intervals of about 3¼ cm (1½ in), but do not cut right through the bread. Spread soft butter generously between the un-separated slices. Crush 1 or 2 cloves of garlic, chop very finely, and distribute among the slashes. Or you may mix the garlic with the butter before spreading. Wrap the bread in aluminium foil, and place in a medium oven, 350°F, Regulo 4, for 10 to 15 minutes. Unwrap, and serve very hot.

Ravioli

450 g (1 lb) flour   *water*
2 or 3 eggs   *forcemeat*
salt

Pour the flour in a mound on a very large pastry board or the marble top of a large table. Make a well in the flour and break into it 2 eggs. Add a teaspoonful of salt and 4 table-spoonsful of water. Pull the dry ingredients into the wet ones, and knead until you can tell whether or not you should add the third egg. The paste should be fairly solid, but not unmanageably so. Continue kneading it and pushing it until it acquires elasticity. Flour your hands and the board and the rolling pin frequently to avoid sticking. Divide the paste in half and roll out the first half, wrapping it around the rolling pin and stretching it with each roll. After about 10 rolls, it will be thin and much enlarged, but roll it further until you can see the grain of the wooden pastry board through it. Lay it over a clean cloth across the back of a chair, and roll out the other half. Let the sheets rest on separate cloths for 30 minutes before filling. Spread one sheet out flat on your board, and put little mounds of chicken, foie gras or other forcemeat at regular intervals about 3 cm (1¼ in) apart. Lay the second sheet loosely over the first. With a small ravioli cutter, cut out the individual ravioli, pressing hard so that the edges are well closed. Put them on a floured cloth in one layer only until time to cook them. Cover them with a second floured cloth. They will keep for a day or so under refrigeration. When ready to cook, slide them into gently boiling salted water, and cook gently for about 4 minutes, until they rise to the surface. Lift them out with a slotted spoon, and add to clear soup at the last minute.

Royale

This garnish is composed of a mixture of clear meat stock, variously flavoured, thickened with eggs and baked in small moulds in a bain-marie in the oven. The moulds must be well buttered before the mixture is put in, and the cooked royale should be quite cold before it is turned out. When turned out, the royale is diced or cut into shapes with a pastry cutter. They are used especially as a garnish for clear soups. The quantities given are for 1¾ litres (3 pints) soup. The water in the bain-marie should not boil, and the royales should be baked at 375° F, Regulo 5, for about 35 minutes if in large moulds; 15 minutes if in small ones.

Plain Royale

Put a large pinch of chervil into 140 ml (¼ pint) boiling clear meat stock, and leave it to infuse for 10 minutes. Beat lightly 1 whole egg and 2 yolks. Blend the egg mixture little by little into the stock. Strain, skim and pour into buttered moulds. Cook as directed above.

Royale à la Crécy

Thinly slice 1 medium carrot, and cook slowly in butter with a seasoning of salt and a pinch of sugar until tender. Add 2 teaspoons Béchamel sauce, and 2 tablespoons cream, and put through a sieve or blend. Blend in 4 egg yolks, pour into a buttered mould, and cook as directed above.

Chicken Royale

Pound to a pulp 2 tablespoons cooked white meat of chicken. Add 2 tablespoons Béchamel sauce, and 2 tablespoons cream, and sieve or blend. Blend in 4 egg yolks, and poach as directed above.

Saint-Germain Royale

Blend 2 heaped tablespoons fresh pea purée with 4 table-spoons clear meat stock. Season with salt and a little sugar. Blend in 1 whole egg and 2 yolks. Pour into a mould and poach as directed above.

Royale of Tomato Purée

Thin 70 ml (½ gill) very red concentrated tomato purée with 4 tablespoons clear meat stock. Season with salt and sugar, thicken with 4 egg yolks, and poach as directed above.

Gnocchi

75 g (2½ oz) butter	*2 teaspoons flour*
85 g (3 oz) semolina	*salt*
1 egg	*grated nutmeg*

Put the butter into a bowl and cream it until soft. Work in the lightly beaten egg, the semolina and the flour. Season with the salt and nutmeg. Work vigorously with a spatula until the mixture is slightly frothy. Let it stand for an hour. Shape large oval balls out of the mixture with a tablespoon. Place the balls into a buttered pan as you make them. When ready to cook, pour boiling water over them and simmer for 20 minutes.

Spun Eggs

Beat 1 egg as for omelette. Strain it through a sieve. Put it into a fine conical strainer and, holding the strainer over boiling clear stock, wave it back and forth over the stock as you force the egg through. The egg will coagulate in threads as it enters the boiling liquid. Drain the egg threads carefully and add them to the soup just before serving.

Tomato Garnish

Peel, drain and seed some small firm tomatoes. Dice the flesh into ½ cm (¼ in) dice, and add to boiling clear meat stock. Simmer for 7 minutes. Drain, and add to the soup.

Liver Dumplings for Soup

450 g (1 lb) calf's liver	*parsley*
1 slice of bread	*salt and pepper*
110 g (4 oz) beef suet	*thyme*
4 egg yolks	*bay leaf*
2 egg whites	*60 g (2 oz) dried breadcrumbs*

Remove skin and tubes from the liver, and chop it finely. This will be easier if you first soak it for ½ hour in milk. Soak the bread in stock or in the liver milk. Squeeze the bread. Mix the chopped liver and the bread, herbs, seasoning and very finely chopped suet. Beat the egg yolks and the 2 whites together and add to the liver mixture. Sprinkle in a bit of the breadcrumbs, and form a sample dumpling the size of an egg yolk. With a wet spoon, lower it into boiling broth and simmer for 8 minutes. If too soft, add more breadcrumbs; if too solid, add another egg yolk. When you have a sample of just the right consistency, cook them all in stock, and serve 3 or 4 per person in a soup plate of bouillon.

Marrow Dumplings

beef marrow from 1 kg (2¼ lb) marrow bones	*2 teaspoons finely-chopped parsley*
60–85 g (3–4 oz) dried breadcrumbs	*2 eggs*
	salt and pepper
	flour

After the marrow bones have been used for broth, take out the marrow and chop or mash it. Add 60 g (3 oz) dried breadcrumbs, salt, pepper, parsley and the beaten eggs. If the mixture is not firm enough, add the rest of the breadcrumbs. With floured hands, make the mixture into small dumplings. Roll them in flour and drop them one by one into the marrow broth or stock. They will cook in about 6 minutes – taste after 5 minutes. Ladle some meat or marrow broth into soup bowls, and add a few dumplings to each serving.

Glossary

Bain-marie A vessel containing hot water in which sauces and other delicate dishes can be kept hot in small pans, or in which they may be cooked without the risk of curdling or separation. In U.S.A. cookery; a double boiler.

Beurre manié Kneaded butter and flour, used as a thickening agent. As a general guide, use 22½ g (¾ oz) butter to 30 g (1 oz) flour.

Déglacer (deglaze) To dilute the concentrated juices in a pan in which meat, poultry, game or fish has been roasted. Red or white wine, Madeira, clear soup, stock or cream are generally used for this purpose.

Julienne A term used in French cookery to designate any foodstuffs coarsely or finely shredded.

Mirepoix A mixture of diced vegetables, occasionally mixed with diced raw ham or blanched pork belly, used to enhance the flavour of meat, fish, poultry or shellfish dishes.

Béchamel Sauce

280 ml (½ pint) milk	*23 g (¾ oz) butter*
a slice of onion	*23 g (¾ oz) flour*
6 peppercorns	*salt*
a blade of mace	*pepper*
a bay leaf	

Add the onion, herbs and spices to the milk. Cover the pan, and set over low heat to infuse for 5 to 7 minutes. Do not boil. In another saucepan, melt the butter, stir in the flour until well blended, and strain on one-third of the milk. Blend well and gradually add the remainder. When well blended, season lightly, return to the heat, and stir continually until boiling. Boil for 1 or 2 minutes, then adjust the seasoning.

Velouté Sauce

23 g (¾ oz) butter
23 g (¾ oz) flour
210 ml (1½ gills) fish, vegetable
or meat stock

70 ml (½ gill) creamy milk
salt
pepper
few drops of lemon juice

Melt the butter, stir in the flour, and cook over low heat for a minute or two, until pale straw colour. Draw aside. Pour on the stock, blend, return to the heat, and stir until the mixture begins to thicken. Season and add the milk. Bring to the boil, stirring, and simmer for several minutes, until thick and smooth. Draw aside and stir in the lemon juice.

Bibliography

Aromas and Flavors of Past and Present, Alice B. Toklas, Harper & Brothers, N.Y., 1958.

Au Petit Cordon Bleu, Dione Lucas and Rosemary Hume, J. M. Dent and Sons Ltd., 1953.

The Constance Spry Cookery Book, Constance Spry and Rosemary Hume, J. M. Dent and Sons Ltd., 1964.

Cooking for Pleasure, Rupert Croft-Cooke, William Collins Sons & Co., Ltd., 1963.

Encyclopedia of European Cooking, edited by Musia Soper, Spring Books, Paul Hamlyn Ltd., 1969.

The Englishman's Food, J. C. Drummond and Anne Wilbraham, Jonathan Cape, 1964.

Fish Cookery, Jane Grigson, Penguin Books Ltd., 1975.

French Provincial Cooking, Elizabeth David, Michael Joseph, 1960.

The Gentle Art of Cookery, Mrs. C. F. Leyel and Miss Olga Hartley, Chatto and Windus, 1925.

Good Things, Jane Grigson, Penguin Books Ltd., 1973.

Great Dishes of the World, Robert Carrier, Sphere Books Ltd., 1967.

The Joy of Cooking, Irma S. Rombauer, Marion Rombauer Becker, The Bobbs-Merrill Company, Inc., New York, 1953.

Larousse Gastronomique, Prosper Montagné, Paul Hamlyn Ltd., 1961.

Mastering the Art of French Cooking, Simone Beck, Louisette Bertholle, Julia Child, Penguin Books Ltd., 1966.

Modern Cookery for Private Families, Eliza Acton, Elek Books Ltd., 1966.

Penguin Cordon Bleu Cookery, Rosemary Hume and Muriel Downes, Penguin Books Ltd., 1963.

Plats du Jour, Patience Gray and Primrose Boyd, Penguin Books Ltd., 1957.

Soups and Hors d'Oeuvres, Marika Hanbury-Tenison, Penguin Books Ltd., 1969.

Sunset Cook Book of Soups & Stews, Lane Books, Menlo Park, California, 1971.

The New Vegetable Grower's Handbook, Arthur J. Simons, Penguin Books Ltd., 1975.

Harold Wilshaw, *The Guardian*.

Index

Other non-fiction available from Magnum Books

These and other Magnum Books are available at your bookshop or newsagent. In case of difficulties orders may be sent to:

Magnum Books
Cash Sales Department
P.O. Box 11
Falmouth
Cornwall TR10 10gEN

Please send cheque or postal order, no currency, for purchase price quoted and allow the following for postage and packing:

U.K. 19p for the first book plus 9p per copy for each additional book ordered, to a maximum of 73p.

B.F.P.O. & Eire 19p for the first book plus 9p per copy for the next 6 books, thereafter 3p per book.

Overseas Customers 20p for the first book and 10p per copy for each additional book.

While every effort is made to keep prices low, it is sometimes necessary to increase prices at short notice. Magnum Books reserve the right to show new retail prices on covers which may differ from those previously advertised in the text or elsewhere.